MELANIE,

AND

Other Poems.

C. Harding Pinxt G. Parker Sculpt

Yours very truly
N. P. Willis

M E L A N I E

AND

Other Poems.

BY N. P. WILLIS.

"Pray pardon me;
For I am like a boy that hath found money,
Afraid I dream still."

WEBSTER.

SECOND EDITION.

NEW YORK:
SAUNDERS AND OTLEY, ANN STREET,
MDCCCXXXVII.

CRAIGHEAD AND ALLEN,
PRINTERS,
NO. 112 FULTON, CORNER OF DUTCH STREET.

TO

THE REV. LOUIS DWIGHT,

This Volume

IS AFFECTIONATELY INSCRIBED,

BY HIS KINSMAN,

THE AUTHOR.

CONTENTS.

MELANIE.

I.

I stood on yonder rocky brow,*
  And marvell'd at the Sybil's fane,
When I was not what I am now.
  My life was then untouch'd of pain;
And, as the breeze that stirr'd my hair,
  My spirit freshened in the sky,
And all things that were true and fair
  Lay closely to my loving eye,
With nothing shadowy between—
I was a boy of seventeen.
Yon wondrous temple crests the rock,
  As light upon its giddy base,

* The story is told during a walk around the Cascatelles of Tivoli.

As stirless with the torrent's shock,
  As pure in its proportioned grace,
And seems a thing of air, as then,
Afloat above this fairy glen;
  But though mine eye will kindle still
In looking on the shapes of art,
  The link is lost that sent the thrill,
Like lightning, instant to my heart.
And thus may break before we die,
Th' electric chain 'twixt soul and eye!

Ten years—like yon bright valley, sown
  Alternately with weeds and flowers—
Had swiftly, if not gaily, flown,
  And still I lov'd the rosy Hours;
And if there lurk'd within my breast
  Some nerve that had been overstrung
And quiver'd in my hours of rest,
  Like bells by their own echo rung,
I was with Hope a masquer yet,
  And well could hide the look of sadness
And, if my heart would not forget,
  I knew, at least, the trick of gladness,

And when another sang the strain,
I mingled in the old refrain.

'Twere idle to remember now,
  Had I the heart, my thwarted schemes.
I bear beneath this alter'd brow
  The ashes of a thousand dreams—
Some wrought of wild Ambition's fingers,
  Some colored of Love's pencil well—
But none of which a shadow lingers,
  And none whose story I could tell.
Enough, that when I climbed again
  To Tivoli's romantic steep,
Life had no joy, and scarce a pain,
  Whose wells I had not tasted deep;
And from my lips the thirst had pass'd
For every fount save one—the sweetest—and the last.
The last—the last! My friends were dead,
  Or false; my mother in her grave;
Above my father's honor'd head
  The sea had lock'd its hiding wave;
Ambition had but foil'd my grasp,
And love had perish'd in my clasp;

And still, I say, I did not slack
My love of life, and hope of pleasure,
But gather'd my affections back;
And, as the miser hugs his treasure
When plague and ruin bid him flee,
I closer clung to mine--my lov'd, lost Melanie!

The last of the De Brevern race,
My sister claimed no kinsman's care;
And, looking from each other's face,
The eye stole upward unaware—
For there was nought whereon to lean
Each other's heart and heaven between—
Yet that was world enough for me,
And, for a brief but blessed while,
There seemed no care for Melanie
If she could see her brother smile;
But life with her was at the flow,
And every wave went sparkling higher,
While mine was ebbing, fast and low,
From the same shore of vain desire,
And knew I, with prophetic heart,
That we were wearing aye insensibly apart.

II.

We came to Italy. I felt
A yearning for its sunny sky;
My very spirit seem'd to melt
As swept its first warm breezes by.
From lip and cheek a chilling mist,
From life and soul a frozen rime,
By every breath seem'd softly kiss'd—
God's blessing on its radiant clime!
It was an endless joy to me
To see my sister's new delight;
From Venice in its golden sea
To Pœstum in its purple light,
By sweet Val d'Arno's tinted hills,
In Vallombrosa's convent gloom,
Mid Terni's vale of singing rills,
By deathless lairs in solemn Rome,
In gay Palermo's "Golden Shell,"
At Arethusa's hidden well—
We loiter'd like th' impassion'd sun
That slept so lovingly on all,
And made a home of every one—

Ruin, and fane, and waterfall—
  And crown'd the dying day with glory
If we had seen, since morn, but one old haunt of story.

We came with Spring to Tivoli.
  My sister lov'd its laughing air
And merry waters, though, for me,
My heart was in another key,
  And sometimes I could scarcely bear
The mirth of their eternal play,
  And, like a child that longs for home
When weary of its holiday,
  I sighed for melancholy Rome.
Perhaps—the fancy haunts me still—
'Twas but a boding sense of ill.

It was a morn, of such a day
  As might have dawn'd on Eden first,
Early in the Italian May.
  Vine-leaf and flower had newly burst,
And on the burthen of the air
The breath of buds came faint and rare;
  And far in the transparent sky

The small, earth-keeping birds were seen
  Soaring deliriously high ;
And through the clefts of newer green
  Yon waters dash'd their living pearls ;
And with a gayer smile and bow
  Troop'd on the merry village girls ;
And from the Contadino's brow
  The low-slouch'd hat was backward thrown,
  With air that scarcely seem'd his own ;
And Melanie, with lips apart,
  And claspéd hands upon my arm,
Flung open her impassion'd heart,
  And bless'd life's mere and breathing charm,
And sang old songs, and gather'd flowers,
And passionately bless'd once more life's
    thrilling hours.

In happiness and idleness
  We wandered down yon sunny vale—
Oh mocking eyes !—a golden tress
  Floats back upon this summer gale !
A foot is tripping on the grass !
  A laugh rings merry in mine ear !

I see a bounding shadow pass!—
O God! my sister *once* was here!
Come with me, friend!—We rested yon!
There grew a flower she pluck'd and wore!
She sat upon this mossy stone!—
That broken fountain running o'er
With the same ring, like silver bells.
She listen'd to its babbling flow,
And said, "Perhaps the gossip tells
Some fountain-nymph's love-story now!"
And as her laugh rang clear and wild,
A youth—a painter—passed and smiled.

He gave the greeting of the morn
With voice that lingered in mine ear.
I knew him sad and gentle born
By those two words so calm and clear.
His frame was slight, his forehead high
And swept by threads of raven hair,
The fire of thought was in his eye,
And he was pale and marble fair,
And Grecian chisel never caught
The soul in those slight features wrought.

I watch'd his graceful step of pride,
Till hidden by yon leaning tree,
And lov'd him ere the echo died;
And so, alas! did Melanie!

We sat and watch'd the fount awhile
In silence, but our thoughts were one;
And then arose, and with a smile
Of sympathy, we saunter'd on;
And she by sudden fits was gay,
And then her laughter died away,
And in this changefulness of mood,
Forgotten now those May-day spells,
We turn'd where Varro's villa stood
And gazing on the Cascatelles,
(Whose hurrying waters wild and white
Seem madden'd as they burst to light)
I chanced to turn my eyes away,
And lo! upon a bank alone,
The youthful painter, sleeping, lay!
His pencils on the grass were thrown,
And by his side a sketch was flung,
And near him as I lightly crept,

To see the picture as he slept,
Upon his feet he lightly sprung;
And gazing with a wild surprise
Upon the face of Melanie,
He said—and dropp'd his earnest eyes—
"Forgive me! but I dream'd of thee!"
His sketch, the while, was in my hand,
And, for the lines I look'd to trace—
A torrent by a palace spann'd,
Half-classic and half fairy-land—
I only found—my sister's face!

III.

Our life was changed. Another love
In its lone woof began to twine;
But ah! the golden thread was wove
Between my sister's heart and mine!
She who had liv'd for me before—
She who had smiled for me alone—
Would live and smile for me no more!
The echo to my heart was gone!
It seemed to me the very skies
Had shone through those averted eyes;

The air had breath'd of balm—the flower
Of radiant beauty seemed to be—
But as *she* lov'd them, hour by hour,
And murmur'd of that love to *me!*
Oh, though it be so heavenly high
The selfishness of earth above,
That, of the watchers in the sky,
He sleeps who guards a brother's love—
Though to a sister's present weal
The deep devotion far transcends
The utmost that the soul can feel
For even its own higher ends—
Though next to God, and more than heaven
For his own sake, he loves her, even—
'Tis difficult to see another,
A passing stranger of a day
Who never hath been friend or brother,
Pluck with a look her heart away—
To see the fair, unsullied brow,
Ne'er kiss'd before without a prayer,
Upon a stranger's bosom now,
Who for the boon took little care—
Who is enrich'd, he knows not why—

Who suddenly hath found a treasure
  Golconda were too poor to buy,
And he, perhaps, too cold to measure—
(Albeit, in her forgetful dream,
Th' unconscious idol happier seem,)
  'Tis difficult at once to crush
The rebel mourner in the breast,
  To press the heart to earth and hush
Its bitter jealousy to rest—
  And difficult—the eye gets dim,
  The lip wants power—to smile on him!

I thank sweet Mary Mother now,
  Who gave me strength those pangs to hide,
And touch'd mine eyes and lit my brow
  With sunshine that my heart belied.
I never spoke of wealth or race
  To one who ask'd so much from me—
I looked but in my sister's face,
  And mus'd if she would happier be;
And hour by hour, and day by day,
  I lov'd the gentle painter more,
  And in the same soft measure wore

My selfish jealousy away;
  And I began to watch his mood,
And feel with her love's trembling care,
  And bade God bless him as he woo'd
That loving girl so fond and fair,
  And on my mind would sometimes press
  A fear that she might love him less.

But Melanie—I little dream'd
  What spells the stirring heart may move—
Pygmalion's statue never seem'd
  More changed with life, than she with love.
The pearl tint of the early dawn
  Flush'd into day-spring's rosy hue—
The meek, moss-folded bud of morn
  Flung open to the light and dew—
The first and half-seen star of even
Wax'd clear amid the deepening heaven—
  Similitudes perchance may be,
But these are changes oftener seen,
  And do not image half to me
My sister's change of face and mien.

'Twas written in her very air
That Love had passed and enter'd there.

IV.

A calm and lovely paradise
Is Italy, for minds at ease.
The sadness of its sunny skies
Weighs not upon the lives of these.
The ruin'd aisle, the crumbling fane,
The broken column, vast and prone,
It may be joy—it may be pain—
Amid such wrecks to walk alone!
The saddest man will sadder be,
The gentlest lover gentler there,
As if, whate'er the spirit's key,
It strengthened in that solemn air.

The heart soon grows to mournful things,
And Italy has not a breeze
But comes on melancholy wings;
And even her majestic trees
Stand ghost-like in the Cæsar's home,
As if their conscious roots were set

In the old graves of giant Rome,
  And drew their sap all kingly yet!
And every stone your feet beneath
  Is broken from some mighty thought,
And sculptures in the dust still breathe
  The fire with which their lines were wrought,
And sunder'd arch, and plunder'd tomb
Still thunder back the echo, "Rome!"

Yet gaily o'er Egeria's fount
  The ivy flings its emerald veil,
And flowers grow fair on Numa's mount,
  And light-sprung arches span the dale,
And soft, from Caracalla's Baths,
  The herdsman's song comes down the breeze
While climb his goats the giddy paths
  To grass-grown architrave and frieze;
And gracefully Albano's hill
  Curves into the horizon's line,
And sweetly sings that classic rill,
  And fairly stands that nameless shrine,
And here, oh, many a sultry noon
And starry eve, that happy June,

Came Angelo and Melanie,
And earth for us was all in tune—
For while Love talk'd with them, Hope walked apart with me!

V.

I shrink from the embittered close
Of my own melancholy tale.
'Tis long since I have waked my woes—
And nerve and voice together fail!
The throb beats faster at my brow,
My brain feels warm with starting tears,
And I shall weep—but heed not thou!
'Twill soothe awhile the ache of years.
The heart transfix'd—worn out with grief—
Will turn the arrow for relief.
The painter was a child of shame!
It stirr'd my pride to know it first,
For I had question'd but his name,
And thought, alas! I knew the worst,
Believing him unknown and poor.
His blood, indeed, was not obscure;
A high-born Conti was his mother,

But, though he knew one parent's face,
He never had beheld the other,
Nor knew his country or his race.
The Roman hid his daughter's shame
Within St. Mona's convent wall,
And gave the boy a painter's name—
And little else to live withal!
And, with a noble's high desires
For ever mounting in his heart,
The boy consum'd with hidden fires,
But wrought in silence at his art;
And sometimes at St. Mona's shrine,
Worn thin with penance harsh and long,
He saw his mother's form divine,
And lov'd her for their mutual wrong.
I said my pride was stirr'd—but no!
The voice that told its bitter tale
Was touch'd so mournfully with wo,
And, as he ceas'd, all deathly pale,
He loos'd the hand of Melanie,
And gaz'd so gaspingly on me—
The demon in my bosom died!

"Not thine," I said, "another's guilt;
  I break no hearts for silly pride;
So, kiss yon weeper if thou wilt!"

VI.

St. Mona's morning mass was done.
  The shrine-lamps struggled with the day;
And rising slowly, one by one,
  Stole the last worshippers away.
The organist played out the hymn,
  The incense, to St. Mary swung,
Had mounted to the cherubim,
  Or to the pillars thinly clung;
And boyish chorister replaced
  The missal that was read no more,
And clos'd, with half irreverent haste,
  Confessional and chancel door;
And as, through aisle and oriel pane,
  The sun wore round his slanting beam,
The dying martyr stirr'd again,
  And warriors battled in its gleam;
And costly tomb and sculptur'd knight
Show'd warm and wondrous in the light.

I have not said that Melanie
    Was radiantly fair—
This earth again may never see
    A loveliness so rare!
She glided up St. Mona's aisle
    That morning as a bride,
And, full as was my heart the while,
    I bless'd her in my pride!
The fountain may not fail the less
    Whose sands are golden ore,
And a sister for her loveliness,
    May not be lov'd the more;
But as, the fount's full heart beneath,
    Those golden sparkles shine,
My sister's beauty seem'd to breathe
    Its brightness over mine!

St. Mona has a chapel dim
    Within the altar's fretted pale,
Where faintly comes the swelling hymn,
    And dies, half lost, the anthem's wail.
And here, in twilight meet for prayer,
    A single lamp hangs o'er the shrine,

And Raphael's Mary, soft and fair,
  Looks down with sweetness half divine,
And here St. Mona's nuns alway
Through lattic'd bars are seen to pray.

Avé and sacrament were o'er,
  And Angelo and Melanie
Still knelt the holy shrine before;
  But prayer, that morn was not for me!
My heart was lock'd! The lip might stir,
  The frame might agonize—and yet,
Oh God! I could not pray for *her!*
  A seal upon my soul was set—
My brow was hot—my brain opprest—
And fiends seem'd muttering round, "Your bridal is unblest!"

With forehead to the lattice laid,
  And thin, white fingers straining through,
A nun the while had softly pray'd.
  Oh, ev'n in prayer that voice I knew!
Each faltering word—each mournful tone—
  Each pleading cadence, half-suppress'd—

Such music had its like alone
  On lips that stole it at her breast!
And ere the orison was done
I lov'd the mother as the son!

And now, the marriage vows to hear,
  The nun unveil'd her brow—
When, sudden, to my startled ear,
There crept a whisper, hoarse like fear,
  "*De Brevern! is it thou!*"
The priest let fall the golden ring,
  The bridegroom stood aghast,
While, like some weird and frantic thing,
  The nun was muttering fast;
And as, in dread, I nearer drew,
She thrust her arms the lattice through,
And held me to her straining view—
  But suddenly begun
To steal upon her brain a light
That stagger'd soul, and sense, and sight,
And, with a mouth all ashy white,
  She shriek'd, "*It is his son!*
The bridegroom is thy blood—thy brother!

Rodolph de Brevern wrong'd his mother!"
And, as that doom of love was heard,
My sister sunk—and died—without a sign or word!

* * *

I shed no tear for her. She died
With her last sunshine in her eyes.
Earth held for her no joy beside
The hope just shatter'd—and she lies
In a green nook of yonder dell;
And near her, in a newer bed,
Her lover—brother—sleeps as well!
Peace to the broken-hearted dead!

LORD IVON AND HIS DAUGHTER.

" Dost thou despise
A love like *this!* A lady should not scorn
One soul that loves her, howe'er lowly it be."

BARRY CORNWALL.

LORD IVON.

How beautiful it is! Come here, my daughter!
Is't not a face of most bewildering brightness?

ISIDORE.

The features are all fair, sir, but so cold—
I could not love such beauty!

LORD IVON.

Yet, ev'n so
Look'd thy lost mother, Isidore! Her brow
Lofty like this—her lips thus delicate,
Yet icy cold in their slight vermeil threads—
Her neck thus queenly, and the sweeping curve
Thus matchless, from the small and "pearl round ear"
To the o'er-polished shoulder. Never swan
Dreamed on the water with a grace so calm!

ISIDORE.

And was she proud, sir?

LORD IVON.

Or I had not loved her.

ISIDORE.

Then runs my lesson wrong. I ever read
Pride was unlovely.

LORD IVON.

Dost thou prate already
Of books, my little one? Nay, then, 'tis time

That a sad tale were told thee. Is thy bird
Fed for the day? Canst thou forget the rein
Of thy beloved Arabian for an hour,
And, the first time in all thy sunny life,
Take sadness to thy heart? Wilt listen, sweet?

ISIDORE.

Hang I not ever on thy lips, dear father?

LORD IVON.

As thou didst enter, I was musing here
Upon this picture. 'Tis the face of one
I never knew; but, for its glorious pride,
I bought it of the painter. There has hung
Ever the cunning curse upon my soul
To love this look in woman. Not the flower
Of all Arcadia, in the Age of Gold,
Look'd she a shepherdess, would be to me
More than the birds are. As th' astrologer
Worships the half-seen star that in its sphere
Dreams not of him, and tramples on the lily
That flings, unask'd, its fragrance in his way,

Yet both (as are the high-born and the low)
Wrought of the same fine Hand—so, daringly,
Flew my boy-hopes beyond me. You are here
In a brave palace, Isidore! The gem
That sparkles in your hair imprisons light
Drunk in the flaming Orient; and gold
Waits on the bidding of those girlish lips
In measure that Aladdin never knew
Yet was I—lowly born!

ISIDORE.

Lord Ivon!

LORD IVON.

Ay,
You wonder; but I tell you that the Lord
Of this tall palace was a peasant's child!
And, looking sometimes on his fair domain,
Thy sire bethinks him of a sickly boy,
Nursed by his mother on a mountain side,
His only wealth a book of poetry,
With which he daily crept into the sun,
To cheat sharp pains with the bewildering dream
Of beauty he had only read of there.

ISIDORE.

Have you the volume still, sir?

LORD IVON.

'Twas the gift
Of a poor scholar wandering in the hills,
Who pitied my sick idleness. I fed
My inmost soul upon the witching rhyme—
A silly tale of a low minstrel boy,
Who broke his heart in singing at a bridal.

ISIDORE.

Loved he the lady, sir?

LORD IVON.

So ran the tale.
How well I do remember it!

ISIDORE.

Alas!
Poor youth!.

LORD IVON.

I never thought to *pity* him.

The bride was a duke's sister; and I mused
Upon the wonder of his daring love,
Till my heart changed within me. I became
Restless and sad; and in my sleep I saw
Beautiful dames all scornfully go by;
And one o'er-weary morn I crept away
Into the glen, and, flung upon a rock,
Over a torrent whose swift, giddy waters
Fill'd me with energy, I swore my soul
To better that false vision, if there were
Manhood or fire within my wretched frame.
I turn'd me homeward with the sunset hour,
Changed—for the thought had conquer'd ev'n
disease;
And my poor mother check'd her busy wheel,
To wonder at the step with which I came.

Oh, heavens! that soft and dewy April eve,
When, in a minstrel's garb, but with a heart
As lofty as the marble shafts upreared
Beneath the stately portico, I stood
At this same palace door!

ISIDORE.

Our own! and you
A minstrel boy!

LORD IVON.

Yes—I had wandered far
Since I shook of my sickness in the hills,
And, with some cunning on the lute, had learn'd
A subtler lesson than humility
In the quick school of want. A menial stood
By the Egyptian sphinx; and when I came
And pray'd to sing beneath the balcony
A song of love for a fair lady's ear,
He insolently bade me to begone.
Listening not, I swept my fingers o'er
The strings in prelude, when the base-born slave
Struck me!

ISIDORE.

Impossible!

LORD IVON.

I dash'd my lute

Into his face, and o'er the threshold flew ;
And, threading rapidly the lofty rooms,
Sought vainly for his master. Suddenly
A wing rushed o'er me, and a radiant girl,
Young as myself, but fairer than the dream
Of my most wild imagining, sprang forth,
Chasing a dove, that, 'wilder'd with pursuit,
Dropt breathless on my bosom.

ISIDORE.

Nay, dear father!
Was't so indeed?

LORD IVON.

I thank'd my blessed star!
And, as the fair, transcendent creature stood
Silent with wonder, I resign'd the bird
To her white hands : and, with a rapid thought,
And lips already eloquent of love,
Turn'd the strange chance to a similitude
Of my own story. Her slight, haughty lip
Curl'd at the warm recital of my wrong,
And on the ivory oval of her cheek
The rose flush'd outward with a deeper red ;

And from that hour the minstrel was at home,
And horse and hound were his, and none might
cross
The minion of the noble Lady Clare.
Art weary of my tale?

ISIDORE.

Dear father!

LORD IVON.

Well!
A summer, and a winter, and a spring,
Went over me like brief and noteless hours.
Forever at the side of one who grew
With every morn more beautiful; the slave,
Willing and quick, of every idle whim;
Singing for no one's bidding but her own,
And then a song from my own passionate heart,
Sung with a lip of fire, but ever named
As an old rhyme that I had chanced to hear;
Riding beside her, sleeping at her door,
Doing her maddest bidding at the risk
Of life—what marvel if at last I grew
Presumptuous?

A messenger one morn
Spurr'd through the gate—"A revel at the court!
And many minstrels, come from many lands,
Will try their harps in presence of the king;
And 'tis the royal pleasure that my lord
Come with the young and lovely Lady Clare,
Rob'd as the queen of Faery, who shall crown
The victor with his bays."

Pass over all
To that bewildering day. She sat enthroned
Amid the court; and never twilight star
Sprang with such sweet surprise upon the eye
As she with her rare beauty on the gaze
Of the gay multitude. The minstrels changed
Their studied songs, and chose her for a theme;
And ever at the pause all eyes upturn'd
And fed upon her loveliness.

The last
Long lay was ended, and the silent crowd
Waited the king's award—when suddenly
The sharp strings of a lyre were swept without,

And a clear voice claim'd hearing for a bard
Belated on his journey. Mask'd, and clad
In a long stole, the herald led me in,
A thousand eyes were on me : but I saw
The new-throned queen, in her high place, alone;
And, kneeling at her feet, I pressed my brow
Upon her footstool, till the images
Of my past hours rush'd thick upon my brain ;
Then, rising hastily, I struck my lyre ;
And, in a story woven of my own,
I so did paint her in her loveliness—
Pouring my heart all out upon the lines
I knew too faithfully, and lavishing
The hoarded fire of a whole age of love
Upon each passionate word, that, as I sunk
Exhausted at the close, the ravish'd crowd
Flung gold and flowers on my still quivering
lyre ;
And the moved monarch in his gladness swore
There was no boon beneath his kingly crown
Too high for such a minstrel!

Did my star

Speak in my fainting ear? Heard I the king?
Or did the audible pulses of my heart
Seem to me so articulate? I rose,
And tore my mask away; and, as the stole
Dropped from my shoulders, I glanced hurriedly
A look upon the face of Lady Clare.
It was enough! I saw that she was changed—
That a brief hour had chilled the open child
To calculating woman—that she read
With cold displeasure my o'er-daring thought;
And on that brow, to me as legible
As stars to the rapt Arab, I could trace
The scorn that waited on me! Sick of life,
Yet, even then, with a half-rallied hope
Prompting my faltering tongue, I blindly knelt,
And claimed the king's fair promise—

ISIDORE.

For the hand
Of Lady Clare?

LORD IVON.

No, sweet one—for a sword.

ISIDORE.

You surely spoke to her?

LORD IVON.

I saw her face
No more for years. I went unto the wars;
And when again I sought that palace door,
A glory heralded the minstrel boy
That monarchs might have envied.

ISIDORE.

Was she there?

LORD IVON.

Yes—and, O God! how beautiful! The last,
The ripest seal of loveliness, was set
Upon her form; and the all-glorious pride
That I had worshipped on her girlish lip,
When her scared dove fled to me, was matured
Into a queenly grace; and nobleness
Was bound like a tiara to her brow,
And every motion breathed of it. There lived
Nothing on earth so ravishingly fair.

ISIDORE.

And you still lov'd her?

LORD IVON.

I had peril'd life
In every shape—had battled on the sea,
And burnt upon the desert, and outgone
Spirits most mad for glory, with this one
O'ermastering hope upon me. Honor, fame,
Gold, even, were as dust beneath my feet;
And war was my disgust, though I had sought
Its horrors like a bloodhound—for her praise.
My life was drunk up with the love of her.

ISIDORE.

And *now* she scorn'd you not?

LORD IVON.

Worse, Isidore!
She pitied me! I did not need a voice
To tell my love. She knew her sometime
minion—
And felt that she should never be adored

With such idolatry as his, and sighed
That hearts so true beat not in palaces—
But I was poor, with all my bright renown,
And lowly born ; and she—the Lady Clare!

ISIDORE.

She could not tell you this?

LORD IVON.

She broke my heart
As kindly as the fisher hooks the worm—
Pitying me the while!

ISIDORE.

And you—

LORD IVON.

Lived on!
But the remembrance irks me, and my throat
Chokes with the utterance!

ISIDORE.

Dear father!

LORD IVON.

Nay—
Thanks to sweet Mary Mother, it is past:
And in this world I shall have no more need
To speak of it.

ISIDORE.

But there were brighter days
In store. My mother and this palace—

LORD IVON.

You outrun
My tale, dear Isidore! But 'tis as well.
I would not linger on it.

Twenty years
From this heart-broken hour, I stood again
An old man and a stranger, at the door
Of this same palace. I had been a slave
For gold that time. My star had wrought with me!
And I was richer than the wizard king
Throned in the mines of Ind. I could not look
On my innumerable gems, the glare

Pained so my sun-struck eyes. My gold was countless.

ISIDORE.

And Lady Clare?

LORD IVON.

I met upon the threshold
Her very self—all youth, all loveliness—
So like the fresh-kept picture in my brain,
That for a moment I forgot all else,
And stagger'd back and wept. She passed me by
With a cold look—

ISIDORE.

Oh! not the Lady Clare!

LORD IVON.

Her daughter yet herself! But what a change
Waited me here! My thin and grizzled locks
Were fairer now than the young minstrel's curls;
My sun-burnt visage and contracted eye
Than the gay soldier in his gallant mien;

My words were wit, my looks interpreted,
And Lady Clare—I tell you, Lady Clare
Leaned fondly—fondly! on my wasted arm.
O God! how changed my nature with all this!
I, that had been all love and tenderness,—
The truest and most gentle heart, till now
That ever beat—grew suddenly a devil!
I bought me lands, and titles, and received
Men's homage wiih a smooth hypocrisy;
And—you will scarce believe me, Isidore—
I suffered them to wile their peerless daughter,
The image and the pride of Lady Clare,
To wed me!

ISIDORE.

Sir! you did not!

LORD IVON.

Ay! I saw
Th' indignant anger when her mother first
Broke the repulsive wish, and the degrees
Of shuddering reluctance as her mind
Admitted the intoxicating tales

Of wealth unlimited. And when she look'd
On my age-stricken features, and my form,
Wasted before its time, and turned away
To hide from me her tears, her very mother
Whispered the cursed comfort in her ear
That made her what she is!

ISIDORE.

You could not wed her,
Knowing all this!

LORD IVON.

I felt that I had lost
My life else. I had wrung, for forty years,
My frame to its last withers; I had flung
My boyhood's fire away—the energy
Of a most sinless youth—the toil, and fret,
And agony of manhood. I had dared,
Fought, suffered, slaved—and never for an hour
Forgot or swerved from my resolve; and now—
With the delirious draught upon my lips—
Dash down the cup!

ISIDORE.

Yet *she* had never wronged you!

LORD IVON.

Thou'rt pleading for thy mother, my sweet child!
And angels hear thee. But if she was wrong'd,
The sin be on the pride that sells its blood
Coldly and only for this damning gold.
Had I not offered youth first? Came I not
With my hands brimm'd with glory to buy love—
And was I not denied?

ISIDORE.

Yet, dearest father,
They forced her not to wed?

LORD IVON.

I called her back
Myself from the church threshold, and, before
Her mother and her kinsmen, bade her swear
It was her own free choice to marry me.
I showed her my shrunk hand, and bade her think
If that was like a bridegroom, and beware

Of perjuring her chaste and spotless soul,
If now she loved me not.

ISIDORE.

What said she, sir?

LORD IVON.

Oh! they had made her even as themselves;
And her young heart was colder than the slab
Unsunn'd beneath Pentelicus. She pressed
My withered fingers in her dewy clasp,
And smiled up in my face, and chid "my lord'
For his wlid fancies, and led on!

ISIDORE.

And no
Misgiving at the altar?

LORD IVON.

None! She swore
To love and cherish me till death should part us,
With a voice as clear as mine.

ISIDORE.

And kept it, father!
In mercy tell me so!

LORD IVON.

She lives, my daughter!

* * * * *

Long ere my babe was born, my pride had ebb'd,
And let my heart down to its better founts
Of tenderness. I had no friends—not one!
My love gush'd to my wife. I rack'd my brain
To find her a new pleasure every hour—
Yet not with me—I fear'd to haunt her eye!
Only at night, when she was slumbering
In all her beauty, I would put away
The curtains till the pale night-lamp shone on her,
And watch her through my tears.

One night her lips
Parted as I gazed on them, and the name
Of a young noble, who had been my guest,
Stole forth in broken murmurs. I let fall

The curtains silently, and left her there
To slumber and dream on; and gliding forth
Upon the terrace, knelt to my pale star,
And swore, that if it pleased the God of light
To let me look upon the unborn child
Lying beneath her heart, I would but press
One kiss upon its lips, and take away
The life that was a blight upon her years.

ISIDORE.

I was that child!

LORD IVON.

Yes—and I heard the cry
Of thy small "piping mouth" as 'twere a call
From my remembering star. I waited only
Thy mother's strength to bear the common shock
Of death within the doors. She rose at last,
And, oh! so sweetly pale! And thou, my child
My heart misgave me as I looked upon thee;
But he was ever at her side whose name
She murmur'd in her sleep; and, lingering on
To drink a little of thy sweetness more

Before I died, I watched their stolen love
As she had been my daughter, with a pure,
Passionless joy that I should leave her soon
To love him as she would. I know not how
To tell thee more. * * *
* * Come, sweet! she is not worthy
Of tears like thine and mine. * *
* * * She fled and left me
The very night! The poison was prepared—
And she had been a widow with the morn
Rich as Golconda. As the midnight chimed
My star rose. Gazing on its mounting orb,
I raised the chalice—but a weakness came
Over my heart; and, taking up the lamp,
I glided to her chamber, and remov'd
The curtains for a last, a parting look
Upon my child. * * *
* * * Had she but taken thee,
I could have felt she had a mother's heart,
And drain'd the chalice still. I could not leave
My babe alone in such a heartless world!

ISIDORE.

Thank God! Thank God!

BIRTH-DAY VERSES.

"The heart that we have lain near before our birth is the only one that cannot forget that it hath loved us."

PHILIP SLINGSBY.

My birthday!—Oh beloved mother!
  My heart is with thee o'er the seas.
I did not think to count another
  Before I wept upon thy knees—
Before this scroll of absent years
Was blotted with thy streaming tears.

My own I do not care to check.
  I weep—albeit here alone—

As if I hung upon thy neck,
  As if thy lips were on my own,
As if this full, sad heart of mine,
Were beating closely upon thine.

Four weary years! How looks she now?
  What light is in those tender eyes?
What trace of time has touch'd the brow
  Whose look is borrow'd of the skies
That listen to her nightly prayer?
How is she changed since *he* was there
Who sleeps upon her heart alway—
  Whose name upon her lips is worn—
For whom the night seems made to pray—
  For whom she wakes to pray at morn—
Whose sight is dim, whose heart-strings stir,
Who weeps these tears—to think of *her!*

I know not if my mother's eyes
  Would find me chang'd in slighter things;
I've wandered beneath many skies,
  And tasted of some bitter springs;
And many leaves, once fair and gay,

From youth's full flower have dropp'd away—
But, as these looser leaves depart,
The lessen'd flower gets near the core,
And, when deserted quite, the heart
Takes closer what was dear of yore—
And yearns to those who lov'd it first—
The sunshine and the dew by which its bud was nurst.

Dear mother! dost thou love me yet?
Am I remember'd in my home?
When those I love for joy are met,
Does some one wish that I would come?
Thou *dost*—I *am* belov'd of these!
But, as the schoolboy numbers o'er
Night after night the Pleiades
And finds the stars he found before,
As turns the maiden oft her token,
As counts the miser aye his gold—
So, till life's silver chord is broken,
Would I of thy fond love be told.
My heart is full, mine eyes are wet—
Dear mother! dost thou love thy long-lost wanderer yet?

Oh! when the hour to meet again
  Creeps on, and, speeding o'er the sea,
My heart takes up its lengthen'd chain,
  And, link by link, draws nearer thee—
When land is hailed, and, from the shore,
  Comes off the blessed breath of home,
With fragrance from my mother's door
Of flowers forgotten when I come—
When port is gain'd, and, slowly now,
  The old familiar paths are past,
And, entering, unconscious how,
  I gaze upon thy face at last,
And run to thee, all faint and weak,
And feel thy tears upon my cheek—
  Oh! if my heart break not with joy,
The light of heaven will fairer seem;
  And I shall grow once more a boy:
And, mother!—'twill be like a dream
  That we were parted thus for years—
And once that we have dried our tears,
  How will the days seem long and bright—
To meet thee always with the morn,
  And hear thy blessing every night—

Thy "dearest," thy "first-born!"—
And be no more as now in a strange land, forlorn!

London, January 20th, 1835.

FLORENCE GRAY.

I WAS in Greece. It was the hour of noon
And the Egean wind had dropp'd asleep
Upon Hymettus, and the thymy isles
Of Salamis and Egina lay hung
Like clouds upon the bright and breathless sea.
I had climb'd up the Acropolis at morn,
And hours had fled as time will in a dream
Amidst its deathless ruins—for the air
Is full of spirits in these mighty fanes,
And they walk with you! As it sultrier grew,
I laid me down within a shadow deep
Of a tall column of the Parthenon,
And, in an absent idleness of thought,
I scrawl'd upon the smooth and marble base.

Tell me, O memory, what wrote I there?
The name of a sweet child I knew at Rome!

I was in Asia. 'Twas a peerless night
Upon the plains of Sardis, and the moon,
Touching my eyelids through the wind-stirr'd tent,
Had witch'd me from my slumber. I arose
And silently stole forth, and by the brink
Of "golden Pactolus," where bathe his waters
The bases of Cybele's columns fair,
I paced away the hours. In wakeful mood
I mused upon the storied past awhile,
Watching the moon that with the same mild eye
Had looked upon the mighty Lydian kings
Sleeping around me—Crœsus, who had heap'd
Within that mouldering portico his gold,
And Gyges, buried with his viewless ring
Beneath yon swelling tumulus—and then
I loitered up the valley to a small
And humbler ruin, where the undefiled*

* "Thou hast a few names even in Sardis which have not defiled their garments: and they shall walk with me in white: for they are worthy."—Revelation iii. 4.

Of the Apocalypse their garments kept
Spotless; and crossing with a conscious awe
The broken threshold, to my spirit's eye
It seem'd as if, amid the moonlight, stood
"The angel of the church of Sardis" still!
And I again pass'd onward, and as dawn
Paled the bright morning star, I laid me down
Weary and sad beside the river's brink,
And 'twixt the moonlight and the rose morn,
Wrote with my finger in the "golden sands."
Tell me, O memory, what wrote I there?
The name of the sweet child I knew at Rome!

The dust is old upon my "sandal-shoon,"
And still I am a pilgrim; I have roved
From wild America to spicy Ind,
And worshipp'd at innumerable shrines
Of beauty; and the painter's art, to me,
And sculpture, speak as with a living tongue,
And of dead kingdoms I recal the soul,
Sitting amid their ruins. I have stored
My memory with thoughts that can allay
Fever and sadness, and when life gets dim,

And I am overladen in my years,
Minister to me. But when wearily
The mind gives over toiling, and with eyes
Open but seeing not, and senses all
Lying awake within their chambers dim,
Thought settles like a fountain, still and clear—
Far in its sleeping depths, as 'twere a gem,
Tell me, O memory, what shines so fair?
The face of the sweet child I knew at Rome!

TO ——

"The desire of the moth for the star—
Of the night for the morrow—
The devotion to something afar
From the sphere of our sorrow,"

SHELLEY.

"L'alma, quel che non ha, sogna e figura."

METASTASIO.

As, gazing on the Pleiades,
We count each fair and starry one,
Yet wander from the light of these
To muse upon the Pleiad gone—
As, bending o'er fresh gathered flowers,
The rose's most enchanting hue
Reminds us but of other hours
Whose roses were all lovely too—
So, dearest, when I rove among
The bright ones of this foreign sky,

And mark the smile, and list the song,
  And watch the dancers gliding by,
The fairer still they seem to be,
The more it stirs a thought of thee!

The sad, sweet bells of twilight chime,
  Of many hearts may touch but one,
And so this seeming careless rhyme
  Will whisper to thy heart alone.
I give it to the winds! The bird,
  Let loose, to his far nest will flee,
And love, though breathed but on a word,
  Will find thee, over land and sea.
Though clouds across the sky have driven,
  We trust the star at last will shine,
And like the very light of heaven
  I trust thy love. *Trust thou in mine!*

TO ——

> "Oh, by that little word
> How many thoughts are stirr'd!—
> The last, the last, the last!"

THE star may but a meteor be,
  That breaks upon the stormy night;
And I may err, believing thee
  A spark of heaven's own changeless light!
But if on earth beams aught so fair,
  It seems, of all the lights that shine,
Serenest in its truth, 'tis there,
  Burning in those soft eyes of thine.
Yet long-watch'd stars from heaven have rush'd,
  And long-lov'd friends have dropp'd away,
And mine—my very heart have crush'd!
  And I have hop'd this many a day,
It liv'd no more for love or pain!
But thou hast stirr'd its depths again,

And to its dull, out-wearied ear,
Thy voice of melody has crept,
In tones it cannot choose but hear ;
And now I feel it only slept,
And know, at ev'n thy lightest smile,
It gathered fire and strength the while.

Fail me not thou! This feeling past,
My heart would never rouse again.
Thou art the brightest—but the last!
And if *this* trust, *this* love is vain—
If thou, all peerless as thou art,
Be not less fair than true of heart—
My loves are o'er! The sun will shine
Upon no grave so hush'd as this dark breast of mine.

THE CONFESSIONAL.

"When thou hast met with careless hearts and cold,
Hearts that young love may touch, but never hold
Not changeless, as the loved and left of old—
Remember me—remember me—
I passionately pray of thee!"
LADY E. S. WORTLEY.

I THOUGHT of thee—I thought of thee,
On ocean many a weary night—
When heaved the long and sullen sea,
With only waves and stars in sight.
We stole along by isles of balm,
We furl'd before the coming gale,
We slept amid the breathless calm,
We flew beneath the straining sail—
But thou wert lost for years to me,
And, day and night I thought of thee!
I thought of thee—I thought of thee,
In France—amid the gay saloon,

Where eyes as dark as eyes may be
  Are many as the leaves in June—
Where life is love, and ev'n the air
  Is pregnant with impassion'd thought,
And song and dance and music are
  With one warm meaning only fraught—
My half-snar'd heart broke lightly free,
And with a blush I thought of thee!

I thought of thee—I thought of thee,
  In Florence,—where the fiery hearts
Of Italy are breathed away
  In wonders of the deathless arts;
Where strays the Contadina down
  Val d' Arno with song of old;
Where clime and women seldom frown,
  And life runs over sands of gold;
I stray'd to lone Fiesolé
On many an eve, and thought of thee.

I thought of thee—I thought of thee,
  In Rome,—when on the Palatine
Night left the Cæsar's palace free

To Time's forgetful foot and mine;
Or, on the Coliseum's wall,
When moonlight touch'd the ivied stone,
Reclining, with a thought of all
That o'er this scene has come and gone—
The shades of Rome would start and flee
Unconsciously—I thought of thee.

I thought of thee—I thought of thee,
In Vallombrosa's holy shade,
Where nobles born the friars be,
By life's rude changes humbler made.
Here Milton fram'd his Paradise;
I slept within his very cell;
And, as I clos'd my weary eyes,
I thought the cowl would fit me well—
The cloisters breath'd, it seemed to me,
Of heart's-ease—but I thought of thee.

I thought of thee—I thought of thee,
In Venice,—on a night in June;
When through the city of the sea,
Like dust of silver slept the moon.

Slow turn'd his oar the gondolier,
  And, as the black barks glided by,
The water to my leaning ear
  Bore back the lover's passing sigh—
It was no place alone to be—
I thought of thee—I thought of thee.

I thought of thee—I thought of thee,
  In the Ionian Isles—when straying
With wise Ulysses by the sea—
  Old Homer's songs around me playing;
Or, watching the bewitched caique,
  That o'er the star-lit waters flew,
I listened to the helmsman Greek,
  Who sung the song that Sappho knew—
The poet's spell, the bark, the sea,
All vanished—as I thought of thee.

I thought of thee—I thought of thee,
  In Greece—when rose the Parthenon
Majestic o'er the Egean sea,
  And heroes with it, one by one;
When, in the grove of Academe,

Where Lais and Leontium stray'd
Discussing Plato's mystic theme,
I lay at noontide in the shade—
The Egean wind, the whispering tree,
Had voices—and I thought of thee.

I thought of thee—I thought of thee,
In Asia—on the Dardanelles;
Where swiftly as the waters flee,
Each wave some sweet old story tells;
And, seated by the marble tank
Which sleeps by Ilium's ruins old,
(The fount where peerless Helen drank,
And Venus lav'd her locks of gold,*)
I thrill'd such classic haunts to see,
Yet even here—I thought of thee.

I thought of thee—I thought of thee,
Where glide the Bosphor's lovely waters,
All palace-lined from sea to sea;

* In the Scamander,—before contending for the prize of beauty on Mount Ida. Its head waters fill a beautiful tank near the walls of Troy.

And ever on its shores the daughters
Of the delicious East are seen,
Printing the brink with slipper'd feet,
And oh, the snowy folds between,
What eyes of heaven your glances meet!
Peris of light no fairer be—
Yet—in Stamboul—I thought of thee.

I've thought of thee—I've thought of thee,
Through change that teaches to forget;
Thy face looks up from every sea,
In every star thine eyes are set,
Though roving beneath Orient skies,
Whose golden beauty breathes of rest,
I envy every bird that flies
Into the far and clouded West:
I think of thee—I think of thee!
Oh, dearest! hast thou thought of me?

LINES ON LEAVING EUROPE.

BRIGHT flag at yonder tapering mast!
  Fling out your field of azure blue;
Let star and stripe be westward cast,
  And point as Freedom's eagle flew!
Strain home! oh lithe and quivering spars!
Point home, my country's flag of stars!

The wind blows fair! the vessel feels
  The pressure of the rising breeze,
And, swiftest of a thousand keels,
  She leaps to the careering seas!
Oh, fair, fair cloud of snowy sail,
  In whose white breast I seem to lie,
How oft, when blew this eastern gale,
  I've seen your semblance in the sky,

And long'd, with breaking heart to flee
On such white pinions o'er the sea!

Adieu, oh lands of fame and eld!
  I turn to watch our foamy track,
And thoughts with which I first beheld
  Yon clouded line, come hurrying back;
My lips are dry with vague desire,—
  My cheek once more is hot with joy—
My pulse, my brain, my soul on fire!—
  Oh, what has changed that traveller-boy!
As leaves the ship this dying foam,
His visions fade behind—his weary heart speeds home!

Adieu, oh soft and southern shore,
  Where dwelt the stars long miss'd in heaven!—
Those forms of beauty seen no more,
  Yet once to Art's rapt vision given!
Oh, still th' enamored sun delays,
  And pries through fount and crumbling fane,
To win to his adoring gaze
  Those children of the sky again!
Irradiate beauty, such as never

That light on other earth hath shone,
Hath made this land her home forever ;
  And could I live for this alone—
Were not my birthright brighter far
Than such voluptuous slave's can be—
Held not the West one glorious star
  New-born and blazing for the free—
Soar'd not to heaven our eagle yet—
Rome, with her Helot sons, should teach me to forget!

Adieu, oh fatherland! I see
  Your white cliffs on th' horizon's rim,
And though to freer skies I flee,
  My heart swells, and my eyes are dim!
As knows the dove the task you give her,
  When loosed upon a foreign shore—
As spreads the rain-drop in the river
  In which it may have flowed before—
To England, over vale and mountain,
  My fancy flew from climes more fair—
My blood, that knew its parent fountain,
  Ran warm and fast in England's air.

My mother! in thy prayer to-night
  There come new words and warmer tears!
On long, long darkness breaks the light—
  Comes home the loved, the lost for years!
Sleep safe, oh wave-worn mariner!
  Fear not, to-night, or storm or sea!
The ear of heaven bends low to *her!*
  He comes to shore who sails with me!
The wind-tost spider needs no token
  How stands the tree when lightnings blaze—
And by a thread from heaven unbroken,
  I know my mother lives and prays!

Dear mother! when our lips can speak—
  When first our tears will let us see—
When I can gaze upon thy cheek,
  And thou, with thy dear eyes, on me—
'Twill be a pastime little sad
  To trace what weight time's heavy fingers
Upon each other's forms have had—
  For all may flee, so feeling lingers!
But there's a change, beloved mother!
  To stir far deeper thoughts of thine;

I come—but with me comes another
  To share the heart once only mine!
Thou, on whose thoughts, when sad and lonely,
  One star arose in memory's heaven—
Thou, who hast watch'd *one* treasure only—
  Watered *one* flower with tears at even—
Room in thy heart! The hearth she left
  Is darken'd to lend light to ours!
There are bright flowers of care bereft,
  And hearts that languish more than flowers—
She was their light—their very air—
  Room, mother! in thy heart!—place for her in thy
    prayer!

English Channel, May, 1836.

THE DYING ALCHYMIST.

THE night wind with a desolate moan swept by,
And the old shutters of the turret swung
Screaming upon their hinges, and the moon,
As the torn edges of the clouds flew past,
Struggled aslant the stained and broken panes
So dimly, that the watchful eye of death
Scarcely was conscious when it went and came.

* * * * *

The fire beneath his crucible was low;
Yet still it burned, and ever as his thoughts
Grew insupportable, he raised himself
Upon his wasted arm, and stirred the coals
With difficult energy, and when the rod
Fell from his nerveless fingers, and his eye
Felt faint within its socket, he shrunk back

Upon his pallet, and with unclosed lips
Muttered a curse on death! The silent room
From its dim corners mockingly gave back
His rattling breath; the humming in the fire
Had the distinctness of a knell, and when
Duly the antique horologe beat one,
He drew a phial from beneath his head,
And drank. And instantly his lips compressed,
And with a shudder in his skeleton frame,
He rose with supernatural strength, and sat
Upright, and communed with himself:—

I did not think to die
Till I had finished what I had to do;
I thought to pierce th' eternal secret through
With this my mortal eye;
I felt—Oh God! it seemeth even now
This cannot be the death-dew on my brow.

And yet it is—I feel
Of this dull sickness at my heart afraid;
And in my eyes the death-sparks flash and fade;
And something seems to steal

Over my bosom like a frozen hand,
Binding its pulses with an icy band.

And this is death! But why
Feel I this wild recoil? It cannot be
Th' immortal spirit shuddereth to be free!
Would it not leap to fly,
Like a chain'd eaglet at its parent's call?
I fear—I fear that this poor life is all!

Yet thus to pass away!—
To live but for a hope that mocks at last—
To agonize, to strive, to watch, to fast,
To waste the light of day,
Night's better beauty, feeling, fancy, thought,
All that we have and are—for this—for nought!

Grant me another year,
God of my spirit!—but a day—to win
Something to satisfy this thirst within!
I would *know* something here!
Break for me but one seal that is unbroken!
Speak for me but one word that is unspoken!

Vain—vain!—my brain is turning
With a swift dizziness, and my heart grows sick,
And these hot temple-throbs come fast and thick,
And I am freezing—burning—
Dying! Oh God! if I might only live!
My phial——Ha! it thrills me—I revive.

* * * * *

Ay—were not man to die
He were too glorious for this narrow sphere!
Had he but time to brood on knowledge here—
Could he but train his eye—
Might he but wait the mystic word and hour—
Only his Maker would transcend his power!

Earth has no mineral strange—
Th' illimitable air no hidden wings—
Water no quality in its covert springs,
And fire no power to change—
Seasons no mystery, and stars no spell,
Which the unwasting soul might not compel.

Oh, but for time to track
The upper stars into the pathless sky—

To see th' invisible spirits, eye to eye—
    To hurl the lightning back—
To tread unhurt the sea's dim-lighted halls—
To chase Day's chariot to the horizon-walls—

    And more, much more—for now
The life-sealed fountains of my nature move—
To nurse and purify this human love—
    To clear the god-like brow
Of weakness and mistrust, and bow it down
Worthy and beautiful, to the much-loved one—

    This were indeed to feel
The soul-thirst slaken at the living stream—
To live—Oh God! that life is but a dream!
    And death——Aha! I reel—
Dim—dim—I faint—darkness comes o'er my eye—
Cover me! save me!——God of heaven! I die!

'Twas morning, and the old man lay alone.
No friend had closed his eyelids, and his lips,
Open and ashy pale, th' expression wore
Of his death-struggle. His long silvery hair

Lay on his hollow temples thin and wild,
His frame was wasted, and his features wan
And haggard as with want, and in his palm
His nails were driven deep, as if the throe
Of the last agony had wrung him sore.

The storm was raging still. The shutters swung
Screaming as harshly in the fitful wind,
And all without went on—as aye it will,
Sunshine or tempest, reckless that a heart
Is breaking, or has broken in its change.

The fire beneath the crucible was out;
The vessels of his mystic art lay round,
Useless and cold as the ambitious hand
That fashioned them, and the small silver rod,
Familiar to his touch for threescore years,
Lay on th' alembic's rim, as if it still
Might vex the elements at its master's will.

And thus had passed from its unequal frame
A soul of fire—a sun-bent eagle stricken
From his high soaring down—an instrument

Broken with its own compass. Oh how poor
Seems the rich gift of genius, when it lies,
Like the adventurous bird that hath out-flown
His strength upon the sea, ambition-wrecked—
A thing the thrush might pity, as she sits
Brooding in quiet on her lowly nest.

THE LEPER.

"Room for the leper! Room!" And, as he came,
The cry passed on—"Room for the leper! Room!"
Sunrise was slanting on the city gates
Rosy and beautiful, and from the hills
The early risen poor were coming in
Duly and cheerfully to their toil, and up
Rose the sharp hammer's clink, and the far hum
Of moving wheels and multitudes astir,
And all that in a city murmur swells,
Unheard but by the watcher's weary ear,
Aching with night's dull silence, or the sick
Hailing the welcome light, and sounds that chase
The death-like images of the dark away.

"Room for the leper!" And aside they stood—
Matron, and child, and pitiless manhood—all
Who met him on his way—and let him pass.
And onward through the open gate he came,
A leper with the ashes on his brow,
Sackcloth about his loins, and on his lip
A covering, stepping painfully and slow,
And with a difficult utterance, like one
Whose heart is with an iron nerve put down,
Crying "Unclean! Unclean!"

'Twas now the first
Of the Judean Autumn, and the leaves
Whose shadows lay so still upon his path,
Had put their beauty forth beneath the eye
Of Judah's loftiest noble. He was young,
And eminently beautiful, and life
Mantled in eloquent fulness on his lip,
And sparkled in his glance, and in his mien
There was a gracious pride that every eye
Followed with benisons—and this was he!
With the soft airs of Summer there had come
A torpor on his frame, which not the speed

Of his best barb, nor music, nor the blast
Of the bold huntsman's horn, nor aught that stirs
The spirit to its bent, might drive away.
The blood beat not as wont within his veins;
Dimness crept o'er his eye; a drowsy sloth
Fetter'd his limbs like palsy, and his mien
With all its loftiness, seemed struck with eld.
Even his voice was changed—a languid moan
Taking the place of the clear, silver key;
And brain and sense grew faint, as if the light,
And very air, were steeped in sluggishness.
He strove with it awhile, as manhood will,
Ever too proud for weakness, till the rein
Slackened within his grasp, and in its poise
The arrowy jereed like an aspen shook.
Day after day, he lay, as if in sleep.
His skin grew dry and bloodless, and white scales
Circled with livid purple, covered him.
And then his nails grew black, and fell away
From the dull flesh about them, and the hues
Deepened beneath the hard unmoistened scales,
And from their edges grew the rank white hair,
—And Helon was a leper!

Day was breaking
When at the altar of the temple stood
The holy priest of God. The incense lamp
Burned with a struggling light, and a low chaunt
Swelled through the hollow arches of the roof
Like an articulate wail, and there, alone,
Wasted to ghastly thinness, Helon knelt.
The echoes of the melancholy strain
Died in the distant aisles, and he rose up,
Struggling with weakness, and bowed down his head
Unto the sprinkled ashes, and put off
His costly raiment for the leper's garb,
And with the sackcloth round him, and his lip
Hid in a loathsome covering, stood still
Waiting to hear his doom :—

Depart! depart, O child
Of Israel, from the temple of thy God!
For He has smote thee with his chastening rod,
And to the desert-wild,
From all thou lov'st away thy feet must flee,
That from thy plague His people may be free.

Depart! and come not near
The busy mart, the crowded city, more;
Nor set thy foot a human threshold o'er;
And stay thou not to hear
Voices that call thee in the way; and fly
From all who in the wilderness pass by.

Wet not thy burning lip
In streams that to a human dwelling glide;
Nor rest thee where the covert fountains hide;
Nor kneel thee down to dip
The water where the pilgrim bends to drink,
By desert well or river's grassy brink.

And pass thou not between
The weary traveller and the cooling breeze;
And lie not down to sleep beneath the trees
Where human tracks are seen;
Nor milk the goat that browseth on the plain,
Nor pluck the standing corn, or yellow grain.

And now depart! and when
Thine heart is heavy, and thine eyes are dim,

Lift up thy prayer beseechingly to Him
Who, from the tribes of men,
Selected thee to feel his chastening rod.
Depart! O leper! and forget not God!

And he went forth—alone! not one of all
The many whom he loved, nor she whose name
Was woven in the fibres of the heart
Breaking within him now, to come and speak
Comfort unto him. Yea—he went his way,
Sick, and heart-broken, and alone—to die!
For God had cursed the leper!

It was noon,
And Helon knelt beside a stagnant pool
In the lone wilderness, and bathed his brow,
Hot with the burning leprosy, and touched
The loathsome water to his fevered lips,
Praying that he might be so blest—to die!
Footsteps approached, and with no strength to flee,
He drew the covering closer on his lip,
Crying "Unclean! unclean!" and in the folds
Of the coarse sackcloth shrouding up his face,

He fell upon the earth till they should pass.
Nearer the stranger came, and bending o'er
The leper's prostrate form, pronounced his name.
"Helon!"—the voice was like the master-tone
Of a rich instrument—most strangely sweet;
And the dull pulses of disease awoke,
And for a moment beat beneath the hot
And leprous scales with a restoring thrill.
"Helon! arise!" and he forgot his curse,
And rose and stood before him.

Love and awe
Mingled in the regard of Helon's eye
As he beheld the stranger. He was not
In costly raiment clad, nor on his brow
The symbol of a princely lineage wore;
No followers at his back, nor in his hand
Buckler, or sword, or spear—yet in his mien
Command sat throned serene, and if he smiled,
A kingly condescension graced his lips,
The lion would have crouched to, in his lair.
His garb was simple, and his sandals worn;
His stature modelled with a perfect grace;

His countenance the impress of a God
Touched with the open innocence of a child;
His eye was blue and calm, as is the sky
In the serenest noon; his hair unshorn
Fell to his shoulders; and his curling beard
The fulness of perfected manhood bore.
He looked on Helon earnestly awhile,
As if his heart was moved, and, stooping down,
He took a little water in his hand
And laid it on his brow, and said, "Be clean!"
And lo! the scales fell from him, and his blood
Coursed with delicious coolness through his veins,
And his dry palms grew moist, and on his brow
The dewy softness of an infant's stole.
His leprosy was cleansed, and he fell down
Prostrate at Jesus' feet and worshiped him.

PARRHASIUS.

"Parrhasius, a painter of Athens, amongst those Olynthian captives Philip of Macedon brought home to sell, bought one very old man; and when he had him at his house, put him to death with extreme torture and torment, the better, by his example, to expres the pains and passions of his Prometheus, whom he was then about to paint."

BURTON'S ANAT. OF MEL.

THERE stood an unsold captive in the mart,
A gray-haired and majestical old man,
Chained to a pillar. It was almost night,
And the last seller from his place had gone,
And not a sound was heard but of a dog
Crunching beneath the stall a refuse bone,
Or the dull echo from the pavement rung,
As the faint captive changed his weary feet.

He had stood there since morning, and borne
From every eye in Athens the cold gaze
Of curious scorn. The Jew had taunted him
For an Olynthian slave. The buyer came
And roughly struck his palm upon his breast,
And touched his unhealed wounds, and with a sneer
Passed on, and when, with weariness o'erspent,
He bowed his head in a forgetful sleep,
Th' inhuman soldier smote him, and with threats
Of torture to his children summoned back
The ebbing blood into his pallid face.

'Twas evening, and the half descended sun
Tipped with a golden fire the many domes
Of Athens, and a yellow atmosphere
Lay rich and dusky in the shaded street
Through which the captive gazed. He had borne up
With a stout heart that long and weary day,
Haughtily patient of his many wrongs,
But now he was alone, and from his nerves
The needless strength departed, and he leaned
Prone on his massy chain, and let his thoughts
Throng on him as they would. Unmarked of him,

Parrhasius at the nearest pillar stood,
Gazing upon his grief. Th' Athenian's cheek
Flush'd as he measured with a painter's eye
The moving picture. The abandon'd limbs,
Stained with the oozing blood, were laced with veins
Swollen to purple fulness; the gray hair,
Thin and disordered, hung about his eyes,
And as a thought of wilder bitterness
Rose in his memory, his lips grew white,
And the fast workings of his bloodless face
Told what a tooth of fire was at his heart.

* * * *

The golden light into the painter's room
Streamed richly, and the hidden colors stole
From the dark pictures radiantly forth,
And in the soft and dewy atmosphere
Like forms and landscapes magical they lay.
The walls were hung with armor, and about
In the dim corners stood the sculptured forms
Of Cytheris, and Dian, and stern Jove,
And from the casement soberly away
Fell the grotesque long shadows, full and true,
And, like a veil of filmy mellowness,
The lint-specks floated in the twilight air.

Parrhasius stood, gazing forgetfully
Upon his canvas. There Prometheus lay,
Chained to the cold rocks of Mount Caucasus,
The vulture at his vitals, and the links
Of the lame Lemnian festering in his flesh,
And as the painter's mind felt through the dim,
Rapt mystery, and plucked the shadows forth
With its far-reaching fancy, and with form
And color clad them, his fine, earnest eye,
Flashed with a passionate fire, and the quick curl
Of his thin nostril, and his quivering lip
Were like the winged God's, breathing from his flight.

"Bring me the captive now!
My hands feels skilful, and the shadows lift
From my waked spirit airily and swift,
And I could paint the bow
Upon the bended heavens—around me play
Colors of such divinity to-day.

Ha! bind him on his back!
Look! as Prometheus in my picture here!
Quick—or he faints!—stand with the cordial near!

Now—bend him to the rack!
Press down the poison'd links into his flesh!
And tear agape that healing wound afresh!

So—let him writhe! How long
Will he live thus? Quick, my good pencil, now!
What a fine agony works upon his brow!
Ha! gray-haired, and so strong!
How fearfully he stifles that short moan!
Gods! if I could but paint a dying groan!

'Pity' thee! So I do!
I pity the dumb victim at the altar—
But does the rob'd priest for his *pity* falter?
I'd rack thee though I knew
A thousand lives were perishing in thine—
What were ten thousand to a fame like mine?

"Hereafter!" Ay—*hereafter!*
A whip to keep a coward to his track!
What gave death ever from his kingdom back
To check the sceptic's laughter?
Come from the grave to-morrow with that story
And I may take some softer path to glory.

No, no, old man! we die
Ev'n as the flowers, and we shall breathe away
Our life upon the chance wind, ev'n as they!
Strain well thy fainting eye—
For when that bloodshot quivering is o'er,
The light of heaven will never reach thee more.

Yet there's a deathless *name!*
A spirit that the smothering vault shall spurn,
And like a steadfast planet mount and burn—
And though its crown of flame
Consumed my brain to ashes as it shone,
By all the fiery stars! I'd bind it on!

Ay—though it bid me rifle
My heart's last fount for its insatiate thirst—
Though every life-strung nerve be maddened first—
Though it should bid me stifle
The yearning in my throat for my sweet child,
And taunt its mother till my brain went wild—

All—I would do it all—
Sooner than die, like a dull worm, to rot—

Thrust foully into the earth to be forgot!
Oh Heavens—but I appal
Your heart, old man! forgive——ha! on your lives
Let him not faint!—rack him till he revives!

Vain—vain—give o'er! His eye
Glazes apace. He does not feel you now—
Stand back! I'll paint the death-dew on his brow!
Gods! if he do not die
But for *one* moment—one—till I eclipse
Conception with the scorn of those calm lips!

Shivering! Hark! he mutters
Brokenly now—that was a difficult breath—
Another? Wilt thou never come, oh, Death!
Look! how his temple flutters!
Is his heart still? Aha! lift up his head!
He shudders--gasps--Jove help him!--so--he's dead."

* * * * * *

How like a mounting devil in the heart
Rules the unreined ambition! Let it once
But play the monarch, and its haughty brow
Glows with a beauty that bewilders thought

And unthrones peace for ever. Putting on
The very pomp of Lucifer, it turns
The heart to ashes, and with not a spring
Left in the bosom for the spirit's lip,
We look upon our splendor and forget
The thirst of which we perish! Yet hath life
Many a falser idol. There are hopes
Promising well, and love-touch'd dreams for some,
And passions, many a wild one, and fair schemes
For gold and pleasure—yet will only this
Balk not the soul—Ambition only gives
Even of bitterness a beaker *full!*
Friendship is but a slow-awaking dream,
Troubled at best—Love is a lamp unseen,
Burning to waste, or, if its light is found,
Nursed for an idle hour, then idly broken—
Gain is a grovelling care, and Folly tires,
And Quiet is a hunger never fed—
And from Love's very bosom, and from Gain,
Or Folly, or a Friend, or from Repose,
From all but keen Ambition, will the soul
Snatch the first moment of forgetfulness
To wander like a restless child away.

Oh, if there were not better hopes than these—
Were there no palm beyond a feverish fame—
If the proud wealth flung back upon the heart
Must canker in its coffers—if the links
Falsehood hath broken will unite no more—
If the deep-yearning love that hath not found
Its like in the cold world, must waste in tears—
If truth, and fervor, and devotedness,
Finding no worthy altar, must return
And die of their own fulness—if beyond
The grave there is no Heaven in whose wide air
The spirit may find room, and in the love
Of whose bright habitants the lavish heart
May spend itself—*what thrice-mocked fools are we!*

THE WIFE'S APPEAL.

"Love borrows greatly from opinion. Pride above all things strengthens affection."

E. L. BULWER.

He sat and read. A book with silver clasps,
All gorgeous with illuminated lines
Of gold and crimson, lay upon a frame
Before him. 'Twas a volume of old time;
And in it were fine mysteries of the stars
Solved with a cunning wisdom, and strange thoughts,
Half prophecy, half poetry, and dreams
Clearer than truth, and speculations wild
That touched the secrets of your very soul,
They were so based on Nature. With a face
Glowing with thought, he pored upon the book.
The cushions of an Indian loom lay soft
Beneath his limbs, and, as he turned the page,

The sunlight, streaming through the curtain's fold,
Fell with a rose-tint on his jewell'd hand,
And the rich woods of the quaint furniture
Lay deepening their veined colours in the sun,
And the stained marbles on the pedestals
Stood like a silent company. Voltaire,
With an infernal sneer upon his lips,
And Socrates, with godlike human love
Stamped on his countenance, and orators
Of times gone by that made them, and old bards,
And Medicean Venus, half divine.
Around the room were shelves of dainty lore,
And rich old pictures hung upon the walls
Where the slant light fell on them; and wrought gems,
Medallions, rare mosaics, and antiques
From Herculaneum, the niches filled.
And on a table of enamel, wrought
With a lost art in Italy, there lay
Prints of fair women, and engravings rare,
And a new poem, and a costly toy,
And in their midst a massive lamp of bronze
Burning sweet spices constantly. Asleep
Upon the carpet couched a graceful hound,

Of a rare breed, and, as his master gave
A murmur of delight at some sweet line,
He raised his slender head, and kept his eye
Upon him till the pleasant smile had passed
From his mild lips, and then he slept again.
The light beyond the crimson folds grew dusk,
And the clear letters of the pleasant book
Mingled and blurred, and the lithe hound rose up,
And, with his earnest eye upon the door,
Listened attentively. It came as wont—
The fall of a light foot upon the stair—
And the fond animal sprang out to meet
His mistress, and caress the ungloved hand,
He seemed to know was beautiful. She stooped
Gracefully down and touched his silken ears
As she passed in—then, with a tenderness,
Half playful and half serious, she knelt
Upon the ottoman and pressed her lips
Upon her husband's forehead.

* * * * *

She rose and put the curtain-folds aside
From the high window, and looked out upon
The shining stars in silence. "Look they not

Like Paradise to thine eye?" he said—
But, as he spoke, a tear fell through the light,
And starting from his seat he folded her
Close to his heart, and, with unsteady voice,
Asked if she was not happy. A faint smile
Broke through her tears; and pushing off the hair
From his fine forehead, she held back his head
With her white hand, and, gazing on his face,
Gave to her heart free utterance:—

Happy?—yes, dearest!—blest
Beyond the limit of my wildest dream—
Too bright, indeed, my blessings ever seem;
There lives not in my breast,
One of Hope's promises by Love unkept,
And yet—forgive me, Ernest—I have wept.

How shall I speak of sadness,
And seem not thankless to my God and thee?
How can the lightest wish but seem to be
The very whim of madness?
Yet, oh, there is a boon thy love beside—
And I will ask it of thee—in my pride!

List, while my boldness lingers!
If thou hadst won yon twinkling star to hear thee—
If thou couldst bid the rainbow's curve bend near
thee—
If thou couldst charm thy fingers
To weave for thee the Sunset's tent of gold—
Wouldst in thine own heart treasure it untold?

If thou hadst Ariel's gift,
To course the veined metals of the earth—
If thou couldst wind a fountain to its birth—
If thou couldst know the drift
Of the lost cloud that sailed into the sky—
Wouldst keep it for thine own unanswered eye?

It is thy life and mine!—
Thou in thyself, and I in thee, misprison
Gifts like a circle of bright stars unrisen—
For thou whose mind should shine
Eminent as a planet's light, art here—
Moved with the starting of a woman's tear!

I have told o'er thy powers
In secret, as a miser tells his gold;

I know thy spirit calm, and true, and bold:
    I've watched thy lightest hours,
And seen thee, in the wildest flush of youth
Touched with the instinct ravishment of truth.

    Thou hast the secret strange
To read that hidden book, the human heart;
Thou hast the ready writer's practised art;
    Thou hast the thought to range
The broadest circles Intellect hath ran—
And thou art God's best work—an honest man!

    And yet thou slumberest here
Like a caged bird that never knew its pinions,
And others track in glory the dominions
    Where thou hast not thy peer—
Setting their weaker eyes unto the sun,
And plucking honor that thou shouldst have won.

    Oh, if thou lov'dst me ever,
Ernest, my husband! If th' idolatry
That lets go heaven to fling its all on thee—
    If to dismiss thee never

In dream or prayer, have given me aught to claim—
Heed me—oh, heed me! and awake to Fame!

Her lips
Closed with an earnest sweetness, and she sat
Gazing into his eyes as if her look
Searched their dark orbs for answer. The warm blood
Into his temples mounted, and across
His countenance the flush of passionate thoughts
Passed with irresolute quickness. He rose up
And paced the dim room rapidly awhile,
Calming his troubled mind, and then he came
And laid his hand upon her orbéd brow,
And in a voice of heavenly tenderness
Answered her:—

Before I knew thee, Mary,
Ambition was my angel. I did hear
For ever its witch'd voices in mine ear;
My days were visionary,
My nights were like the slumbers of the mad,
And every dream swept o'er me glory-clad.

I read the burning letters
Of warlike pomp, on History's page, alone;
I counted nothing the struck widow's moan;
I heard no clank of fetters;
I only felt the trumpet's stirring blast,
And lean-eyed Famine stalked unchallenged past!

I heard with veins of lightning,
The utterance of the Statesman's word of power—
Binding and loosing nations in an hour—
But while my eye was brightening,
A masked detraction breathed upon his fame,
And a curst serpent slimed his written name.

The Poet rapt mine ears
With the transporting music that he sung.
With fibres from his life his lyre he strung,
And bathed the world in tears—
And then he turned away to muse apart,
And scorn stole after him and broke his heart!

Yet here and there I saw
One who did set the world at calm defiance,

And press right onward with a bold reliance ;
And he did seem to awe
The very shadows pressing on his breast,
And, with a strong heart, held himself at rest.

And then I looked again,
And he had shut the door upon the crowd,
And on his face he lay and groaned aloud—
Wrestling with hidden pain ;
And in her chamber sat his wife in tears,
And his sweet babes grew sad with whispered fears.

And so I turn'd sick-hearted
From the bright cup away, and, in my sadness,
Searched mine own bosom for some spring of glad-
ness ;
And lo ! a fountain started
Whose waters ev'n in death flow calm and fast,
And my wild fever-thirst was slaked at last.

And then I met thee, Mary,
And felt how love may into fulness pour,
Like light into a fountain running o'er :

And I did hope to vary
My life but with surprises sweet as this—
A dream, but for thy waking filled with bliss.

Yet now I feel my spirit
Bitterly stirred, and—nay, lift up thy brow!
It is thine own voice echoing to thee now,
And thou didst pray to hear it—
I must unto my work and my stern hours!
Take from my room thy harp, and books and flowers!

* * * * *

* * * * A year—
And in his room again he sat alone.
His frame had lost its fulness in that time;
His manly features had grown sharp and thin,
And from his lips the constant smile had faded.
Wild fires had burned the languor from his eye:
The lids looked fevered, and the brow was bent
With an habitual frown. He was much changed.
His chin was resting on his clenched hand,
And with his foot he beat upon the floor
Unconsciously the time of a sad tune.
Thoughts of the past preyed on him bitterly.

He had won power and held it. He had walked
Steadily upward in the eye of Fame,
And kept his truth unsullied—but his home
Had been invaded by envenomed tongues;
His wife—his spotless wife—had been assailed
By slander, and his child had grown afraid
To come to him—his manner was so stern.
He could not speak beside his own hearth freely.
His friends were half estranged, and vulgar men
Presumed upon their services and grew
Familiar with him. He'd small time to sleep,
And none to pray; and, with his heart in fetters,
He bore deep insults silently, and bowed
Respectfully to men who knew he loathed them!
And when his heart was eloquent with truth,
And love of country and honest zeal
Burned for expression, he could find no words
They would not misinterpret with their lies.
What were his many honors to him now?
The good half doubted, falsehood was so strong—
His home was hateful with its cautious fears—
His wife lay trembling on his very breast
Frighted with calumny!——And this is FAME.

THE SCHOLAR OF THEBET BEN KHORAT.*

"Iufluentia cœli morbum hunc movet, interdum omnibus aliis amotis."

MELANCTHON DE ANIMA, CAP. DE HUMORIBUS.

NIGHT in Arabia. An hour ago,
Pale Dian had descended from the sky,
Flinging her cestus out upon the sea,
And at their watches now the solemn stars
Stood vigilant and lone; and, dead asleep,
With not a shadow moving on its breast,
The breathing earth lay in its silver dew,

* A famous Arabian astrologer, who is said to have spent forty years in discovering the motion of the eighth sphere. He had a scholar, a young Bedouin Arab, who, with a singular passion for knowledge, abandoned his wandering tribe, and, applying himself too closely to astrology, lost his reason and died.

And, trembling on their myriad viewless wings,
Th' imprisoned odors left the flowers to dream
And stole away upon the yielding air.
Ben Khorat's tower stands shadowy and tall
In Mecca's loneliest street; and ever there,
When night is at the deepest, burns his lamp
As constant as the Cynosure, and forth
From his looped window stretch the brazen tubes,
Pointing forever at the central star
Of that dim nebula just lifting now
Over Mount Arafat. The sky to-night
Is of a clearer blackness than is wont,
And far within its depths the colored stars*

* "Even to the naked eye, the stars appear of palpably different colors; but when viewed with a prismatic glass, they may be very accurately classed into the red, the yellow, the brilliant white, the dull white and the anomalous. This is true also of the planets, which shine by reflected light, and of course the difference of color must be supposed to arise from their different powers to absorb and reflect the rays of the sun. The original composition of the stars, and the different dispersive powers of their different atmospheres, may be supposed to account also for this phenomenon."

Sparkle like gems—capricious Antares*
Flushing and paling in the Southern arch,
And azure Lyra, like a woman's eye,
Burning with soft blue lustre, and away
Over the desert the bright Polar-star,
White as a flashing icicle, and here,
Hung like a lamp above th' Arabian sea,
Mars with his dusky glow, and, fairer yet,
Mild Sirius,† tinct with dewy violet,
Set like a flower upon the breast of Eve;
And in the zenith the sweet Pleiades,‡
(Alas—that ev'n a star may pass from heaven
And not be miss'd!)—the linkèd Pleiades
Undimmed are there, though from the sister band
The fairest has gone down, and, South away,
Hirundo|| with its little company,

* This star exhibits a peculiar quality—a rapid and beautiful change in the color of its light; every alternate twinkling being of an intense reddish crimson color, and the answering one of a brilliant white.

† When seen with a prismatic glass, Sirius shows a large brush of exceedingly beautiful violet rays.

‡ The Pleiades are vertical in Arabia.

|| An Arabic constellation placed instead of the Piscis Australis, because the swallow arrives in Arabia about the time of the heliacal rising of the Fishes.

And white-browed Vesta, lamping on her path
Lonely and planet-calm, and, all through heaven,
Articulate almost, they troop to night,
Like unrob'd angels in a prophet's trance.

Ben Khorat knelt before his telescope,*
Gazing with earnest stillness on the stars.
The gray hairs, struggling from his turban folds,
Played with the entering wind upon his cheeks,
And on his breast his venerable beard
With supernatural whiteness loosely fell.
The black flesh swelled about his sandal thongs,
Tight with his painful posture, and his lean
And withered fingers to his knees were clenched,
And the thin lashes of his straining eye
Lay with unwinking closeness to the lens,
Stiffened with tense up-turning. Hour by hour,
Till the stars melted in the flush of morn,
The old astrologer knelt moveless there,
Ravished past pain with the bewildering spheres,

* An anachronism, the author is aware. The Telescope was not invented for a century or two after the time of Ben Khorat.

And, hour by hour, with the same patient thought,
Pored his pale scholar on the characters
Of Chaldee writ, or, as his gaze grew dim
With weariness, the dark-eyed Arab laid
His head upon the window and looked forth
Upon the heavens awhile, until the dews
And the soft beauty of the silent night
Cooled his flushed eyelids, and then patiently
He turned unto his constant task again.

The sparry glinting of the Morning Star
Shot through the leaves of a majestic palm
Fringing Mount Arafat, and, as it caught
The eye of the rapt scholar, he arose
And clasped the volume with an eager haste,
And as the glorious planet mounted on, .
Melting her way into the upper sky,
He breathlessly gazed on her :—

" Star of the silver ray!
Bright as a god, but punctual as a slave—
What spirit the eternal canon gave
That bends thee to thy way?

What is the soul that on thine arrowy light
Is walking earth and heaven in pride to-night?

We know when thou wilt soar
Over the mount—thy change, and place, and
time—
'Tis written in the Chaldee's mystic rhyme
As 'twere a priceless lore!
I knew as much in my Bedouin garb—
Coursing the desert on my flying barb!

How oft amid the tents
Upon Sahara's sands I've walked alone,
Waiting all night for thee, resplendent one!
With what magnificence,
In the last watches, to my thirsting eye,
Thy passionate beauty flushed into the sky!

Oh, God! how flew my soul
Out to thy glory—upward on thy ray—
Panting as thou ascendedst on thy way,
As if thine own control—
This searchless spirit that I cannot find—
Had set its radiant law upon my mind!

More than all stars in heaven
I felt thee in my heart! my love became
A frenzy, and consumed me with its flame.
Ay, in the desert even—
My dark-eyed Abra coursing at my side—
The star, not Abra, was my spirit's bride!

My Abra is no more!
My 'desert-bird' is in a stranger's stall—
My tribe, my tent—I sacrificed them all
For this heart-wasting lore!—
Yet than all these the thought is sweeter far—
Thou wert ascendant at my birth, bright star!

The Chaldee calls me *thine*—
And in this breast, that I must rend to be
A spirit upon wings of light like thee,
I feel that *thou art mine!*
Oh, God! that these dull fetters would give way
And let me forth to track thy silver ray!"

* * * Ben Khorat rose
And silently looked forth upon the East.

The dawn was stealing up into the sky
On its gray feet, the stars grew dim apace,
And faded, till the Morning Star alone,
Soft as a molten diamond's liquid fire,
Burned in the heavens. The morn grew freshlier—
The upper clouds were faintly touched with gold,
The fan-palms rustled in the early air,
Daylight spread cool and broadly to the hills,
And still the star was visible, and still
The young Bedouin with a straining eye
Drank its departing light into his soul.
It faded—melted—and the fiery rim
Of the clear sun came up, and painfully
The passionate scholar pressed upon his eyes
His dusky fingers, and with limbs as weak
As a sick child's, turned fainting to his couch,
And slept. * * *

II.

* * It was the morning watch once more.
The clouds were drifting rapidly above,
And dim and fast the glimmering stars flew through,
And as the fitful gust soughed mournfully,

The shutters shook, and on the sloping roof
Plashed heavily large single drops of rain,
And all was still again. Ben Khorat sat
By the dim lamp, and, while his scholar slept,
Pored on the Chaldee wisdom. At his feet,
Stretched on a pallet, lay the Arab boy,
Muttering fast in his unquiet sleep,
And working his dark fingers in his palms
Convulsively. His sallow lips were pale,
And, as they moved, his teeth showed ghastly through,
White as a charnel bone, and closely drawn
Upon his sunken eyes, as if to press
Some frightful image from the bloodshot balls.
His lids a moment quivered, and again
Relaxed, half open, in a calmer sleep.

Ben Khorat gazed upon the dropping sands
Of the departing hour. The last white grain
Fell through, and with the tremulous hand of age
The old astrologer reversed the glass;
And, as the voiceless monitor went on,
Wasting and wasting with the precious hour,
He looked upon it with a moving lip,

And, starting, turned his gaze upon the heavens.
Cursing the clouds impatiently.

"'Tis time!"
Muttered the dying scholar, and he dashed
The tangled hair from his black eyes away,
And, seizing on Ben Khorat's mantle-folds,
He struggled to his feet, and falling prone
Upon the window-ledge, gazed steadfastly
Into the East:—

"There is a cloud between—
She sits this instant on the mountain's brow,
And that dusk veil hides all her glory now—
Yet floats she as serene
Into the heavens!——Oh, God! that even so
I could o'ermount my spirit-cloud, and go!

The cloud begins to drift!
Aha! Fling open! 'tis the star—the sky!
Touch me, immortal mother! and I fly!
Wider! thou cloudy rift!
Let through!—such glory should have radiant room!
Let through!—a star-child on its light goes home!

Speak to me, brethren bright!
Ye who are floating in these living beams!
Ye who have come to me in starry dreams!
Ye who have winged the light
Of our bright mother with its thoughts of flame—
—(I *knew* it passed through spirits as it came)—

Tell me! what power have ye?
What are the heights ye reach upon your wings?
What know ye of the myriad wondrous things
I perish but to see?
Are ye thought-rapid?—Can ye fly as far—
As instant as a thought, from star to star?

Where has the Pleiad gone?
Where have all missing stars* found light and
home?

* 'Missing stars' are often spoken of in the old books of astronomy. Hipparchus mentions one that appeared and vanished very suddenly; and in the beginning of the sixteenth century Kepler discovered a new star near the heel of the right foot of Serpentarius. "so bright and sparkling that it exceeded any thing he had ever seen before." He "took notice that it was every moment changing into some of the colors of the rainbow,

Who bids the Stella Mira* go and come ?
Why sits the Pole-star lone ?
And why, like banded sisters, through the air
Go in bright troops the constellations fair ?

Ben Khorat ! dost thou mark ?
The star ! the star ! By heavens, the cloud drifts
o'er !
Gone—and I live ! nay—will my heart beat more ?
Look ! master ! 'tis all dark !
Not a clear speck in heaven !—my eye-balls smother !
Break through the clouds once more ! oh, starry
mother !

I will lie down ! Yet, stay,
The rain beats out the odour from the gums,
And strangely soft to-night the spice-wind comes !
I am a child alway

except when it was near the horizon, when it was generally white." It disappeared the following year, and has not been seen since.

* A wonderful star in the neck of the Whale, discovered by Fabricius in the fifteenth century. It appears and disappears seven times in six years, and continues in the greatest lustre for fifteen days together.

When it is on my forehead! Abra sweet!
Would I were in the desert at thy feet!

My barb! my glorious steed!
Methinks my soul would mount upon its track
More fleetly, could I die upon thy back!
How would thy thrilling speed
Quicken my pulse!—Oh, Allah! I get wild!
Would that I were once more a desert-child!

Nay—nay—I had forgot!
My mother! my star mother!—Ha! my breath
Stifles!——more air!——Ben Khorat! this is—death!
Touch me!——I feel you not!
Dying!—Farewell! good master!—room! more room!
Abra! I loved thee! star—bright star! I——come!"

How idly of the human heart we speak,
Giving it gods of clay! How worse than vain
Is the school homily, that Eden's fruit
Cannot be plucked too freely from "the tree
Of good and evil." Wisdom sits alone,
Topmost in heaven;—she is its light—its God!

And in the heart of man she sits as high—
Though grovelling eyes forget her oftentimes,
Seeing but this world's idols. The pure mind
Sees her for ever : and in youth we come
Filled with her sainted ravishment, and kneel,
Worshipping God through her sweet altar-fires,
And then is knowledge "good." We come too oft—
The heart grows proud with fulness, and we soon
Look with licentious freedom on the maid
Throned in celestial beauty. There she sits,
Robed in her soft and seraph loveliness,
Instructing and forgiving, and we gaze
Until desire grows wild, and, with our hands
Upon her very garments, are struck down,
Blasted with a consuming fire from heaven!
Yet, oh! how full of music from her lips
Breathe the calm tones of wisdom! Human praise
Is sweet till envy mars it, and the touch
Of new-won gold stirs up the pulses well,
And woman's love, if in a beggar's lamp
'Twould burn, might light us cheerly through the world;
But Knowledge hath a far more 'wildering tongue,
And she will stoop and lead you to the stars,

And witch you with her mysteries, till gold
Is a forgotten dross, and power and fame
Toys of an hour, and woman's careless love,
Light as the breath that breaks it. He who binds
His soul to knowledge steals the key of heaven—
But 'tis a bitter mockery that the fruit
May hang within his reach, and when, with thirst
Wrought to a maddening frenzy, he would taste—
It burns his lips to ashes!

CHRIST'S ENTRANCE INTO JERUSALEM.

HE sat upon the ass's colt and rode
Toward Jerusalem. Beside him walked
Closely and silently the faithful twelve,
And on before him went a multitude
Shouting Hosannas, and with eager hands
Strewing their garments thickly in his way.
Th' unbroken foal beneath him gently stepp'd,
Tame as its patient dam; and as the song
Of "welcome to the Son of David" burst
Forth from a thousand children, and the leaves
Of the wav'd branches touch'd its silken ears,
It turned its wild eye for a moment back,
And then, subdued by an invisible hand,
Meekly trode onward with its slender feet.

The dew's last sparkle from the grass had gone

As he rode up Mount Olivet. The woods
Threw their cool shadows freshly to the west,
And the light foal, with quick and toiling step
And head bent low, kept its unslacken'd way
Till its soft mane was lifted by the wind
Sent o'er the mount from Jordan. As he reach'd
The summit's breezy pitch, the Saviour rais'd
His calm blue eye—there stood Jerusulem!
Eagerly he bent forward, and beneath
His mantle's passive folds, a bolder line
Than the wont slightness of his perfect limbs
Betray'd the swelling fulness of his heart.
There stood Jerusalem! How fair she look'd—
The silver sun on all her palaces,
And her fair daughters mid the golden spires
Tending their terrace flowers, and Kedron's stream
Lacing the meadows with its silver band,
And wreathing its mist-mantle on the sky
With the morn's exhalations. There she stood—
Jerusalem—the city of his love,
Chosen from all the earth; Jerusalem—
That knew him not—and had rejected him;
Jerusalem—for whom he came to die!

The shouts redoubled from a thousand lips
At the fair sight, the children leap'd and sang
Louder Hosannas; the clear air was filled
With odor from the trampled olive leaves—
—But "Jesus wept." The lov'd disciple saw
His Master's tears, and closer to his side
He came with yearning looks, and on his neck
The Saviour leant with heavenly tenderness,
And mourn'd—"How oft, Jerusalem! would I
Have gather'd you, as gathereth a hen
Her brood beneath her wings—but ye would not!"

He thought not of the death that he should die—
He thought not of the thorns he knew must pierce
His forehead—of the buffet on the cheek—
The scourge, the mocking homage, the foul scorn!—

Gethsemane stood out beneath his eye
Clear in the morning sun, and there, he knew,
While they who "could not watch with him one
hour"
Were sleeping, he should sweat great drops of blood,
Praying the "cup might pass." And Golgotha

Stood bare and desert by the city wall,
And in its midst, to his prophetic eye,
Rose the rough cross, and its keen agonies
Were number'd all—the nails were in his feet—
Th' insulting sponge was pressing on his lips—
The blood and water gushing from his side—
The dizzy faintness swimming in his brain—
And, while his own disciples fled in fear,
A world's death-agonies all mix'd in his!
Ay!—he forgot all this. He only saw
Jerusalem,—the chos'n—the lov'd—the lost!
He only felt that for her sake his life
Was vainly giv'n, and in his pitying love,
The sufferings that would clothe the Heavens in
black,
Were quite forgotten.
Was there ever love,
In earth or heaven equal unto this?

THE HEALING OF THE DAUGHTER OF JAIRUS.*

Freshly the cool breath of the coming eve
Stole through the lattice, and the dying girl
Felt it upon her forehead. She had lain
Since the hot noontide in a breathless trance,
Her thin pale fingers clasp'd within the hand
Of the heart-broken Ruler, and her breast,
Like the dead marble, white and motionless.
The shadow of a leaf lay on her lips,
And as it stirr'd with the awakening wind,
The dark lids lifted from her languid eyes,
And her slight fingers mov'd, and heavily
She turn'd upon her pillow. He was there—
The same lov'd, tireless watcher, and she look'd
Into his face until her sight grew dim

* Luke viii. 54, 55.

With the fast-falling tears, and, with a sigh
Of tremulous weakness, murmuring his name,
She gently drew his hands upon her lips,
And kiss'd it as she wept. The old man sunk
Upon his knees, and in the drapery
Of the rich curtains buried up his face—
And when the twilight fell, the silken folds
Stirr'd with his prayer, but the slight hand he held
Had ceased its pressure, and he could not hear
In the dead, utter silence, that a breath
Came through her nostrils, and her temples gave
To his nice touch no pulse, and at her mouth
He held the lightest curl that on her neck
Lay with a mocking beauty, and his gaze
Ach'd with its deathly stillness. . .

. . . . It was night—
And softly o'er the Sea of Galilee
Danced the breeze-ridden ripples to the shore,
Tipp'd with the silver sparkles of the moon.
The breaking waves play'd low upon the beach
Their constant music, but the air beside
Was still as starlight, and the Saviour's voice,

In its rich cadences unearthly sweet,
Seemed like some just-born harmony in the air,
Wak'd by the power of wisdom. On a rock,
With the broad moonlight falling on his brow,
He stood and taught the people. At his feet
Lay his small scrip, and pilgrim's scallop-shell,
And staff for they had waited by the sea
Till he came o'er from Gadarene, and pray'd
For his wont teachings as he came to land.
His hair was parted meekly on his brow,
And the long curls from off his shoulders fell
As he leaned forward earnestly, and still
The same calm cadence, passionless and deep,
And in his looks the same mild majesty,
And in his mien the sadness mix'd with power,
Fill'd them with love and wonder. Suddenly,
As on his words entrancedly they hung,
The crowd divided, and among them stood
Jairus the Ruler. With his flowing robe
Gather'd in haste about his loins, he came,
And fix'd his eyes on Jesus. Closer drew
The twelve disciples to their Master's side,
And silently the people shrunk away,

And left the haughty Ruler in the midst
Alone. A moment longer on the face
Of the meek Nazarene he kept his gaze,
And as the twelve look'd on him, by the light
Of the clear moon they saw a glistening tear
Steal to his silver beard, and drawing nigh
Unto the Saviour's feet, he took the hem
Of his coarse mantle, and with trembling hands
Press'd it upon his lips, and murmur'd low,
"*Master! my daughter!*"— . . .

. . . . . The same silvery light,
That shone upon the lone rock by the sea,
Slept on the Ruler's lofty capitals
As at the door he stood, and welcom'd in
Jesus and his disciples. All was still.
The echoing vestibule gave back the slide
Of their loose sandals, and the arrowy beam
Of moonlight slanting to the marble floor
Lay like a spell of silence in the rooms
As Jairus led them on. With hushing steps
He trod the winding stair, but ere he touch'd
The latchet, from within a whisper came,

"*Trouble the Master not—for she is dead!*"
And his faint hand fell nerveless at his side,
And his steps falter'd, and his broken voice
Chok'd in its utterance;—But a gentle hand
Was laid upon his arm, and in his ear
The Saviour's voice sank thrillingly and low,
"*She is not dead—but sleepeth.*"

They pass'd in.
The spice-lamps in the alabaster urns
Burn'd dimly, and the white and fragrant smoke
Curl'd indolently on the chamber walls.
The silken curtains slumbered in their folds—
Not ev'n a tassel stirring in the air—
And as the Saviour stood beside the bed,
And pray'd inaudibly, the Ruler heard
The quickening division of his breath
As he grew earnest inwardly. There came
A gradual brightness o'er his calm sad face,
And drawing nearer to the bed, he mov'd
The silken curtains silently apart
And look'd upon the maiden.

Like a form
Of matchless sculpture in her sleep she lay—
The linen vesture folded on her breast,
And over it her white transparent hands,
The blood still rosy in their tapering nails.
A line of pearl ran through her parted lips,
And in her nostrils, spiritually thin,
The breathing curve was mockingly like life,
And round beneath the faintly tinted skin
Ran the light branches of the azure veins—
And on her cheek the jet lash overlay
Matching the arches pencill'd on her brow:
Her hair had been unbound, and falling loose
Upon her pillow, hid her small round ears
In curls of glossy blackness, and about
Her polished neck, scarce touching it, they hung
Like airy shadows floating as they slept.
'Twas heavenly beautiful. The Saviour rais'd
Her hand from off her bosom, and spread out
The snowy fingers in his palm, and said
"*Maiden! Arise!*"—and suddenly a flush
Shot o'er her forehead, and along her lips
And through her cheek the rallied color ran,

And the still outline of her graceful form
Stirr'd in the linen vesture, and she clasp'd
The Saviour's hand, and fixing her dark eyes
Full on his beaming countenance—AROSE !

THE SOLDIER'S WIDOW.

Wo for my vine clad home!
That it should ever be so dark to me,
With its bright threshold, and its whispering tree!
That I should ever come,
Fearing the lonely echo of a tread
Beneath the roof-tree of my glorious dead!

Lead on my orphan boy!
Thy home is not so desolate to thee—
And the low shiver in the linden tree
May bring to thee a joy;
But, oh, how dark is the bright home before thee,
To her who with a joyous spirit bore thee!

Lead on! for thou art now
My sole remaining helper. God hath spoken,
And the strong heart I lean'd upon is broken;
And I have seen his brow,
The forehead of my upright one, and just,
Trod by the hoof of battle to the dust.

He will not meet thee there
Who blest thee at the eventide, my son!
And when the shadows of the night steal on,
He will not call to prayer.
The lips that melted, giving thee to God,
Are in the icy keeping of the sod!

Ay, my own boy! thy sire
Is with the sleepers of the valley cast,
And the proud glory of my life hath past
With his high glance of fire.
Wo that the linden and the vine should bloom,
And a just man be gather'd to the tomb!

Why—bear them proudly, boy!
It is the sword he girded to his thigh—

It is the helm he wore in victory—
    And shall we have no joy?
For thy green vales, oh Switzerland, he died!—
I will forget my sorrow in my pride!

EXTRACT FROM A POEM DELIVERED AT THE DEPARTURE OF THE SENIOR CLASS OF YALE COLLEGE, IN 1826.

*　　*　　*　　*　　*　　*　　*

WE shall go forth together. There will come
Alike the day of trial unto all,
And the rude world will buffet us alike.
Temptation hath a music for all ears;
And mad ambition trumpeteth to all;
And the ungovernable thought within
Will be in every bosom eloquent;—
But, when the silence and the calm come on,
And the high seal of character is set,
We shall not all be similar. The scale
Of being is a graduated thing;
And deeper than the vanities of power,
Or the vain pomp of glory, there is writ

Gradation, in its hidden characters.
The pathway to the grave may be the same,
And the proud man shall tread it, and the low,
With his bowed head, shall bear him company.
Decay will make no difference, and death,
With his cold hand, shall make no difference;
And there will be no precedence of power,
In waking at the coming trump of God;
But in the temper of the invisible mind,
The godlike and undying intellect,
There are distinctions that will live in heaven,
When time is a forgotten circumstance!
The elevated brow of kings will lose
The impress of regalia, and the slave
Will wear his immortality as free,
Beside the crystal waters; but the depth
Of glory in the attributes of God,
Will measure the capacities of mind;
And as the angels differ, will the ken
Of gifted spirits glorify him more.
It is life's mystery. The soul of man
Createth its own destiny of power;
And, as the trial is intenser here,

His being hath a nobler strength in heaven.

What is its earthly victory? Press on!
For it hath tempted angels. Yet press on!
For it shall make you mighty among men;
And from the eyrie of your eagle thought,
Ye shall look down on monarchs. O press on!
For the high ones and powerful shall come
To do you reverence: and the beautiful
Will know the purer language of your brow,
And read it like a talisman of love!
Press on! for it is godlike to unloose
The spirit, and forget yourself in thought;
Bending a pinion for the deeper sky,
And, in the very fetters of your flesh,
Mating with the pure essences of heaven!
Press on!—'for in the grave there is no work,
And no device.'—Press on! while yet ye may!

So lives the soul of man. It is the thirst
Of his immortal nature; and he rends
The rock for secret fountains, and pursues
The path of the illimitable wind

For mysteries—and this is human pride!
There is a gentler element, and man
May breathe it with a calm, unruffled soul,
And drink its living waters till his heart
Is pure—and this is human happiness!
Its secret and its evidence are writ
In the broad book of nature. 'Tis to have
Attentive and believing faculties;
To go abroad rejoicing in the joy
Of beautiful and well created things;
To love the voice of waters, and the sheen
Of silver fountains leaping to the sea;
To thrill with the rich melody of birds,
Living their life of music; to be glad
In the gay sunshine, reverent in the storm;
To see a beauty in the stirring leaf,
And find calm thoughts beneath the whispering tree;
To see, and hear, and breathe the evidence
Of God's deep wisdom in the natural world!
It is to linger on 'the magic face
Of human beauty,' and from light and shade
Alike to draw a lesson; 'tis to love
The cadences of voices that are tuned

By majesty and purity of thought;
To gaze on woman's beauty, as a star
Whose purity and distance make it fair;
And in the gush of music to be still,
And feel that it has purified the heart!
It is to love all virtue for itself,
All nature for its breathing evidence;
And, when the eye hath seen, and when the ear
Hath drunk the beautiful harmony of the world,
It is to humble the imperfect mind,
And lean the broken spirit upon God!

Thus would I, at this parting hour, be true
To the great moral of a passing world.
Thus would I—like a just departing child,
Who lingers on the threshold of his home—
Remember the best lesson of the lips
Whose accents shall be with us now, no more!
It is the gift of sorrow to be pure:
And I would press the lesson; that, when life
Hath half become a weariness, and hope
Thirsts for serener waters, go abroad
Upon the paths of nature, and, when all

Its voices whisper, and its silent things
Are breathing the deep beauty of the world,
Kneel at its simple altar, and the God
Who hath the living waters shall be there!

TO A CITY PIGEON.

Stoop to my window, thou beautiful dove!
Thy daily visits have touch'd my love,
I watch thy coming, and list the note
That stirs so low in thy mellow throat,
    And my joy is high
To catch the glance of thy gentle eye.

Why dost thou sit on the heated eves,
And forsake the wood with its freshen'd leaves?
Why dost thou haunt the sultry street,
When the paths of the forest are cool and sweet?
    How canst thou bear
This noise of people—this sultry air?

Thou alone of the feather'd race
Dost look unscared on the human face;
Thou alone, with a wing to flee,
Dost love with man in his haunts to be;
        And "the gentle dove"
Has become a name for trust and love.

A holy gift is thine, sweet bird!
Thou'rt nam'd with childhood's earliest word!
Thou'rt link'd with all that is fresh and wild
In the prison'd thoughts of the city child,
        And thy glossy wings
Are its brightest image of moving things.

It is no light chance. Thou art set apart,
Wisely by Him who has tam'd thy heart,
To stir the love for the bright and fair
That else were seal'd in this crowded air;
        I sometimes dream
Angelic rays from thy pinions stream.

Come then, ever, when daylight leaves
The page I read, to my humble eaves,

And wash thy breast in the hollow spout,
And murmur thy low sweet music out!
I hear and see
Lessons of Heaven, sweet bird, in thee!

TO JULIA GRISI,

AFTER HEARING HER IN ANNA BOLENA.

When the rose is brightest,
Its bloom will soonest fly;
When burns the meteor lightest,
'Twill vanish from the sky!
If Death but wait until Delight
O'errun the heart like wine,
And break the cup when brimming quite—
I die—for thou hast pour'd, to-night,
The last drop into mine.

THE BAPTISM OF CHRIST.

It was a green spot in the wilderness,
Touch'd by the river Jordan. The dark pine
Never had dropp'd its tassels on the moss
Tufting the leaning bank, nor on the grass
Of the broad circle stretching evenly
To the straight larches, had a heavier foot
Than the wild heron's trodden. Softly in
Through a long aisle of willows, dim and cool,
Stole the clear waters with their muffled feet,
And hushing as they spread into the light,
Circled the edges of the pebbled tank
Slowly, then rippled through the woods away.

Hither had come th' Apostle of the wild,

Winding the river's course. 'Twas near the flush
Of eve, and, with a multitude around,
Who from the cities had come out to hear,
He stood breast high amid the running stream,
Baptizing as the Spirit gave him power.
His simple raiment was of camel's hair,
A leathern girdle close about his loins,
His beard unshorn, and for his daily meat
The locust and wild honey of the wood—
But like the face of Moses on the mount
Shone his rapt countenance, and in his eye
Burned the mild fire of love, as he spoke
The ear lean'd to him, and persuasion swift
To the chain'd spirit of the listener stole.

Silent upon the green and sloping bank
The people sat, and while the leaves were shook
With the birds dropping early to their nests,
And the grey eve came on, within their hearts
They mus'd if he were Christ. The rippling stream
Still turned its silver courses from his breast
As he divined their thought. "I but baptize,"
He said "with water; but there cometh One

The latchet of whose shoes I may not dare
Ev'n to unloose. He will baptize with fire
And with the Holy Ghost." And lo! while yet
The words were on his lips, he rais'd his eyes
And on the bank stood Jesus. He had laid
His raiment off, and with his loins alone
Girt with a mantle, and his perfect limbs,
In their angelic slightness, meek and bare,
He waited to go in. But John forbade,
And hurried to his feet and stay'd him there,
And said, "Nay, Master! I have need of *thine*,
Not thou of *mine!*" And Jesus, with a smile
Of heavenly sadness, met his earnest looks,
And answered, "Suffer it to be so now;
For thus it doth become me to fulfil
All righteousness." And, leaning to the stream,
He took around him the Apostle's arm
And drew him gently to the midst.

The wood
Was thick with the dim twilight as they came
Up from the water. With his clasped hands
Laid on his breast th' Apostle silently

Followed his Master's steps—when lo! a light,
Bright as the tenfold glory of the sun,
Yet lambent as the softly burning stars,
Enveloped them, and from the heavens away
Parted the dim blue ether like a veil;
And as a voice, fearful exceedingly,
Broke from the midst, "THIS IS MY MUCH LOV'D SON
IN WHOM I AM WELL PLEASED," a snow-white dove,
Floating upon its wings, descended thro',
And shedding a swift music from its plumes,
Circled, and flutter'd to the Saviour's breast.

ON A PICTURE OF A BEAUTIFUL BOY.

"Thou who yet dost keep
Thy heritage, thou eye among the blind,
That, deaf and silent, readst the eternal deep,
Haunted for ever by the eternal mind."

WORDSWORTH.

A BOY! yet in his eye you trace
The watchfulness of riper years,
And tales are in that serious face
Of feelings early steep'd in tears;
And in that tranquil gaze
There lingers many a thought unsaid,
Shadows of other days,
Whose hours with shapes of beauty came and fled·

And sometimes it is even so!
The spirit ripens in the germ;
The new-seal'd fountains overflow,
The bright wings tremble in the worm.
The soul detects some passing token,
Some emblem of a brighter world,
And, with its shell of clay unbroken,
Its shining pinions are unfurl'd,
And, like a blessed dream,
Phantoms, apparell'd from the sky,
Athwart its vision gleam
As if the light of Heaven had touched its gifted eye.

'Tis strange how childhood's simple words
Interpret Nature's mystic book—
How it will listen to the birds,
Or ponder on the running brook,
As if its spirit fed.
And strange that we remember not,
Who fill its eye, and weave its lot,
How lightly it were led
Back to the home which it has scarce forgot.

ON THE PICTURE OF A "CHILD TIRED OF PLAY."

Tired of play! Tired of play!
What hast thou done this livelong day?
The birds are silent, and so is the bee;
The sun is creeping up steeple and tree;
The doves have flown to the sheltering eaves,
And the nests are dark with the drooping leaves,
Twilight gathers, and day is done—
How hast thou spent it—restless one!

Playing? But what hast thou done beside
To tell thy mother at even tide?
What promise of morn is left unbroken?

What kind word to thy playmate spoken?
Whom hast thou pitied, and whom forgiven?
How with thy faults has duty striven?
What hast thou learned by field and hill,
By greenwood path, and by singing rill?

There will come an eve to a longer day,
That will find thee tired—but not of play!
And thou wilt lean, as thou leanest now,
With drooping limbs and an aching brow,
And wish the shadows would faster creep,
And long to go to thy quiet sleep.
Well were it then if thine aching brow
Were as free from sin and shame as now!
Well for thee, if thy lip could tell
A tale like this, of a day spent well.
If thine open hand hath reliev'd distress
If thy pity hath sprung to wretchedness—
If thou hast forgiven the sore offence,
And humbled thy heart with penitence—
If Nature's voices have spoken to thee
With their holy meanings eloquently—
If every creature hath won thy love,

From the creeping worm to the brooding dove,
If never a sad, low-spoken word
Hath plead with thy human heart unheard—
Then, when the night steals on as now,
It will bring relief to thine aching brow,
And, with joy and peace at the thought of rest,
Thou wilt sink to sleep on thy mother's breast.

TO A FACE BELOVED.

The music of the waken'd lyre
   Dies not upon the quivering strings,
Nor burns alone the minstrel's fire
   Upon the lip that trembling sings;
Nor shines the moon in heaven unseen,
   Nor shuts the flower its fragrant cells,
Nor sleeps the fountain's wealth, I ween,
   For ever in its sparry wells—
The spells of the enchanter lie
Not on his own lone heart—his own rapt ear and eye.

I look upon a face as fair
   As ever made a lip of heaven

Falter amid its music-prayer!
The first-lit star of summer even
Springs not so softly on the eye,
Nor grows, with watching half so bright,
Nor mid its sisters of the sky,
So seems of heaven the dearest light—
Men murmur where that face is seen,
My youth's angelic dream was of that look and mien.

Yet though we deem the stars are blest,
And envy, in our grief, the flower
That bears but sweetness in its breast,
And feared th' enchanter for his power,
And love the minstrel for his spell,
He winds out of his lyre so well—
The stars are almoners of light,
The lyrist of melodious air,
The fountain of its waters bright
And every thing most sweet and fair
Of that by which it charms the ear,
The eye of him that passes near—
A lamp is lit in woman's eye
That souls, else lost on earth, remember angels by.

IDLENESS.

> "Idleness is sweet and sacred."
>
> WALTER SAVAGE LANDOR.

> "When you have found a day to be idle, be idle for a day.
> "When you have met with three cups to drink, drink your three cups."
>
> CHINESE POET.

THE rain is playing its soft pleasant tune
Fitfully on the skylight, and the shade
Of the fast-flying clouds across my book
Passes with delicate change. My merry fire
Sings cheerfully to itself; my musing cat
Purrs as she wakes from her unquiet sleep,
And looks into my face as if she felt

Like me the gentle influence of the rain.
Here have I sat since morn, reading sometimes,
And sometimes listening to the faster fall
Of the large drops, or rising with the stir
Of an unbidden thought, have walked awhile
With the slow steps of indolence, my room,
And then sat down composedly again
To my quaint book of olden poetry.
It is a kind of idleness, I know ;
And I am said to be an idle man—
And it is very true. I love to go
Out in the pleasant sun, and let my eye
Rest on the human faces that pass by,
Each with its gay or busy interest :
And then I muse upon their lot, and read
Many a lesson in their changeful cast,
And so grow kind of heart, as if the sight
Of human beings were humanity.
And I am better after it, and go
More gratefully to my rest, and feel a love
Stirring my heart to every living thing,
And my low prayer has more humility,
And I sink lightlier to my dreams—and this,

'Tis very true, is only idleness!
I love to go and mingle with the young
In the gay festal room—when every heart
Is beating faster than the merry tune,
And their blue eyes are restless, and their lips
Parted with eager joy, and their round cheeks
Flushed with the beautiful motion of the dance.
And I can look upon such things, and go
Back to my solitude, and dream bright dreams
For their fast coming years, and speak of them
Earnestly in my prayer, till I am glad
With a benevolent joy—and this, I know,
To the world's eye is only idleness!

And when the clouds pass suddenly away,
And the blue sky is like a newer world,
And the sweet growing things—forest and flower,
Humble and beautiful alike—are all
Breathing up odors to the very heaven—
Or when the frost has yielded to the sun
In the rich autumn, and the filmy mist
Lies like a silver lining on the sky,

And the clear air exhilirates, and life
Simply, is luxury—and when the hush
Of twilight, like a gentle sleep, steals on,
And the birds settle to their nests, and stars
Spring in the upper sky, and there is not
A sound that is not low and musical—
At all these pleasant seasons I go out
With my first impulse guiding me, and take
Woodpath or stream, or slope by hill or vale,
And in my recklessness of heart, stray on,
Glad with the birds, and silent with the leaves,
And happy with the fair and blessed world—
And this, 'tis true, is only idleness!

And I should love to go up to the sky,
And course the heavens, like stars, and float away
Upon the gliding clouds that have no stay
In their swift journey—and 'twould be a joy
To walk the chambers of the deep, and tread
The pearls of its untrodden floor, and know
The tribes of the unfathomable depths—
Dwellers beneath the pressure of a sea!

And I should love to issue with the wind
On a strong errand, and o'ersweep the earth
With its broad continents and islands green,
Like to the passing of a spirit on!—
And this, 'tis true, were only idleness!

THE BURIAL OF ARNOLD.

YE'VE gathered to your place of prayer
With slow and meausured tread:
Your ranks are full, your mates all there—
But the soul of one has fled.
He was the proudest in his strength,
The manliest of ye all;
Why lies he at that fearful length,
And ye around his pall?

Ye reckon it in days, since he
Strode up that foot-worn aisle,
With his dark eye flashing gloriously,

And his lip wreathed with a smile.
O, had it been but told you, then,
To mark whose lamp was dim,
From out yon rank of fresh-lipped men,
Would ye have singled him?

Whose was the sinewy arm, that flung
Defiance to the ring?
Whose laugh of victory loudest rung—
Yet not for glorying?
Whose heart, in generous deed and thought,
No rivalry might brook,
And yet distinction claiming not?
There lies he—go and look!

On now—his requiem is done,
The last deep prayer is said—
On to his burial, comrades—on,
With the noblest of the dead!
Slow—for it presses heavily—
It is a man ye bear!
Slow, for our thoughts dwell wearily
On the noble sleeper there.

Tread lightly, comrades!—we have laid
  His dark locks on his brow—
Like life—save deeper light and shade:
  We'll not disturb them now.
Tread lightly—for 'tis beautiful,
  That blue-veined eye-lid's sleep,
Hiding the eye death left so dull—
  Its slumber we will keep.

Rest now!—his journeying is done—
  Your feet are on his sod—
Death's chain is on your champion—
  He waiteth here his God
Ay—turn and weep—'tis manliness
  To be heart-broken here—
For the grave of earth's best nobleness
  Is watered by the tear.

SPRING.

" L'onda del mar divisa
Bagna la valle e l'monte,
    Va passegiera
    In fiume,
    Va prigionera
    In fonte,
Mormora sempre e geme
Finche non torna al mar."

METASTASIO.

THE Spring is here—the delicate-footed May,
  With its slight fingers full of leaves and flowers
And with it comes a thirst to be away,
  Wasting in wood-paths its voluptuous hours—
A feeling that is like a sense of wings,
Restless to soar above these perishing things.

We pass out from the city's feverish hum,
To find refreshment in the silent woods;
And nature, that is beautiful and dumb,
Like a cool sleep upon the pulses broods—
Yet, even there, a restless thought will steal
To teach the indolent heart it still must *feel.*

Strange, that the audible stillness of the noon,
The waters tripping with their silver feet,
The turning to the light leaves in June,
And the light whisper as their edges meet—
Strange—that they fill not, with their tranquil tone,
The spirit, walking in their midst alone.

There's no contentment in a world like this,
Save in forgetting the immortal dream;
We may not gaze upon the stars of bliss,
That through the cloud-rifts radiantly stream;
Bird-like, the prisoned soul *will* lift its eye
And pine till it is hooded from the sky.

THE TORN HAT.

(A PICTURE BY SULLY.)

. . . . . . "A leaf
Fresh flung upon a river, that will dance
Upon the wave that stealeth out its life,
Then sink of its own heaviness."

PHILIP SLINGSBY.

THERE'S something in a noble boy,
A brave, free-hearted, careless one,
With his unchecked, unbidden joy,
His dread of books and love of fun,
And in his clear and ready smile,
Unshaded by a thought of guile,

And unrepressed by sadness—
Which brings me to my childhood back,
As if I trod its very track,
And felt its very gladness.
And yet it is not in his play,
When every trace of thought is lost,
And not when you would call him gay,
That his bright presence thrills me most.
His shout may ring upon the hill,
His voice be echoed in the hall,
His merry laugh like music trill,
And I in sadness hear it all—
For, like the wrinkles on my brow,
I scarcely notice such things now—
But when, amid the earnest game,
He stops, as if he music heard,
And, heedless of his shouted name
As of the carol of a bird,
Stands gazing on the empty air
As if some dream were passing there—
'Tis then that on his face I look,
His beautiful but thoughtful face,
And, like a long-forgotten book,

Its sweet, familiar meanings trace
Remembering a thousand things
Which passed me on those golden wings,
Which time has fettered now—
Things that came o'er me with a thrill,
And left me silent, sad, and still,
And threw upon my brow
A holier and a gentler cast,
That was too innocent to last.

'Tis strange how thought upon a child
Will, like a presence, sometimes press,
And when his pulse is beating wild,
And life itself is in excess—
When foot and hand, and ear and eye,
Are all with ardor straining high—
How in his heart will spring
A feeling whose mysterious thrall
Is stronger, sweeter far than all;
And on its silent wing,
How with the clouds he'll float away,
As wandering and as lost as they!

APRIL.

" A violet by a mossy stone,
 Half hidden from the eye,
Fair as a star, when only one
 Is shining in the sky."
WORDSWORTH.

I HAVE found violets. April hath come on,
And the cool winds feel softer, and the rain
Falls in the beaded drops of summer time.
You may hear birds at morning, and at eve
The tame dove lingers till the twilight falls,
Cooing upon the eaves, and drawing in
His beautiful bright neck, and, from the hills,
A murmur like the hoarseness of the sea

Tells the release of waters, and the earth
Sends up a pleasant smell, and the dry leaves
Are lifted by the grass—and so I know
That Nature, with her delicate ear, hath heard
The dropping of the velvet foot of Spring.
Take of my violets! I found them where
The liquid South stole o'er them, on a bank
That leaned to running water. There's to me
A daintiness about these early flowers
That touches me like poetry. They blow
With such a simple loveliness among
The common herbs of pasture, and breathe out
Their lives so unobtrusively, like hearts
Whose beatings are too gentle for the world.
I love to go in the capricious days
Of April and hunt violets; when the rain
Is in the blue cups trembling, and they nod
So gracefully to the kisses of the wind.
It may be deem'd too idle, but the young
Read nature like the manuscript of heaven,
And call the flowers its poetry. Go out!
Ye spirits of habitual unrest,
And read it when the "fever of the world"

Hath made your hearts impatient, and, if life
Hath yet one spring unpoisoned, it will be
Like a beguiling music to its flow,
And you will no more wonder that I love
To hunt for violets in the April time.

THE BELFRY PIGEON.

"Mine eyes are sick of this perpetual flow
Of people, and my heart of one sad thought."

SHELLEY.

On the cross beam under the Old South bell
The nest of a pigeon is builded well.
In summer and winter that bird is there,
Out and in with the morning air:
I love to see him track the street,
With his wary eye and active feet;
And I often watch him as he springs,
Circling the steeple with easy wings,
Till across the dial his shade has passed,
And the belfry edge is gained at last.

'Tis a bird I love, with its brooding note,
And the trembling throb in its mottled throat;
There's a human look in its swelling breast,
And the gentle curve of its lowly crest;
And I often stop with the fear I feel—
He runs so close to the rapid wheel.

Whatever is rung on that noisy bell—
Chime of the hour or funeral knell—
The dove in the belfry must hear it well.
When the tongue swings out to the midnight moon—
When the sexton cheerly rings for noon—
When the clock strikes clear at morning light—
When the child is waked with "nine at night"—
When the chimes play soft in the Sabbath air,
Filling the spirit with tones of prayer—
Whatever tale in the bell is heard,
He broods on his folded feet unstirred,
Or rising half in his rounded nest,
He takes the time to smooth his breast,
Then drops again with filmed eyes,
And sleeps as the last vibration dies.

Sweet bird! I would that I could be
A hermit in the crowd like thee!
With wings to fly to wood and glen,
Thy lot, like mine, is cast with men;
And daily, with unwilling feet,
I tread, like thee, the crowded street;
But, unlike me, when day is o'er,
Thou canst dismiss the world and soar,
Or, at a half felt wish for rest,
Canst smooth thy feathers on thy breast,
And drop forgetful, to thy nest.

I would that in such wings of gold
I could my weary heart upfold;
I would I could look down unmoved,
(Unloving as I am unloved,)
And while the world throngs on beneath,
Smooth down my cares and calmly breathe;
And never sad with others' sadness,
And never glad with others' gladness,
Listen, unstirred, to knell or chime,
And, lapt in quiet, bide my time.

TO LAURA W——, TWO YEARS OF AGE.

Bright be the skies that cover thee,
  Child of the sunny brow—
Bright as the dream flung over thee—
  By all that meets thee now.
Thy heart is beating joyously,
  Thy voice is like a bird's—
And sweetly breaks the melody
  Of thy imperfect words.
I know no fount that gushes out
As gladly as thy tiny shout.

I would that thou might'st ever be
  As beautiful as now,—

That time might ever leave as free
Thy yet unwritten brow:
I would life were "all poetry"
To gentle measure set,
That nought but chasten'd melody
Might stain thy eye of jet—
Nor one discordant note be spoken,
Till God the cunning harp hath broken.

I would—but deeper things than these
With woman's lot are wove:
Wrought of intenser sympathies,
And nerv'd by purest love—
By the strong spirit's discipline,
By the fierce wrong forgiven,
By all that wrings the heart of sin,
Is woman won to Heaven.
"Her lot is on thee," lovely child—
God keep thy spirit undefiled!

I fear thy gentle loveliness,
Thy witching tone and air,
Thine eye's beseeching earnestness

May be to thee a snare.
The silver stars may purely shine,
The water's taintless flow—
But they who kneel at woman's shrine,
Breathe on it as they bow—
Ye may fling back the gift again,
But the crushed flower will leave a stain.

What shall preserve thee, beautiful child?
Keep thee as thou art now?
Bring thee, a spirit undefiled,
At God's pure throne to bow?
The world is but a broken reed,
And life grows early dim—
Who shall be near thee in thy need,
To lead thee up—to Him?
He, who himself was "undefiled?"
With him, we trust thee, beautiful child!

ON A PICTURE OF A GIRL LEADING HER BLIND MOTHER THROUGH THE WOOD.

The green leaves as we pass
Lay their light fingers on thee unaware,
And by thy side the hazels cluster fair,
And the low forest-grass
Grows green and silken where the wood-paths wind—
Alas! for thee, sweet mother! thou art blind!

And nature is all bright;
And the faint gray and crimson of the dawn,
Like folded curtains from the day are drawn;
And evening's purple light
Quivers in tremulous softness on the sky—
Alas! sweet mother! for thy clouded eye!

The moon's new silver shell
Trembles above thee, and the stars float up,
In the blue air, and the rich tulip's cup
Is pencill'd passing well,
And the swift birds on glorious pinions flee—
Alas! sweet mother! that thou canst not see!

And the kind looks of friends
Peruse the sad expression in thy face,
And the child stops amid his bounding race,
And the tall stripling bends
Low to thine ear with duty unforgot—
Alas! sweet mother! that thou seest them not!

But thou canst *hear!* and love
May richly on a human tone be pour'd,
And the least cadence of a whisper'd word
A daughter's love may prove—
And while I speak thou knowst if I smile,
Albeit thou canst not see my face the while!

Yes, thou canst hear! and He
Who on thy sightless eye its darkness hung,

To the attentive ear, like harps, hath strung
Heaven and earth and sea!
And 'tis a lesson in our hearts to know—
With but one sense the soul may overflow.

TO A STOLEN RING.

Oh for thy history now! Hadst thou a tongue
To whisper of thy secrets, I could lay
Upon thy jewell'd tracery mine ear
And dream myself in heaven. Thou hast been worn
In that fair creature's pride, and thou hast felt
The bounding of the haughtiest blood that e'er
Sprang from the heart of woman; and thy gold
Has lain upon her forehead in the hour
Of sadness, when the weary thoughts came fast
And life was but a bitterness with all
Its vividness and beauty. She has gazed
In her fair girlhood on thy snowy pearls,
And mused away the hours, and she has bent
On thee the downcast radiance of her eye

When a deep tone was eloquent in her ear,
And thou hast lain upon her cheek, and prest
Back on her heart its beatings, and put by
From her vein'd temples the luxuriant curls,
And in her peaceful sleep, when she has lain
In her unconscious beauty, and the dreams
Of her high heart came goldenly and soft,
Thou hast been there unchidden, and hast felt
The swelling of the clear transparent veins
As the rich blood rush'd through them, warm and fast.

I am impatient as I gaze on thee,
Thou inarticulate jewel! Thou hast heard
With thy dull ear such music!—the low tone
Of a young sister's tenderness, when night
Hath folded them together like one flower—
The sudden snatch of a remember'd song
Warbled capriciously—the careless word
Lightly betraying the inaudible thought
Working within the heart, and more than all,
Thou hast been lifted when the fervent prayer
For a lov'd mother, or the sleeping one

Lying beside her, trembled on her lip,
And the warm tear that from her eye stole out
As the soft lash fell over it, has lain,
Amid thy shining jewels like a star.

TO MY MOTHER FROM THE APPENINES.

"Mother! dear mother! the feelings nurst
As I hung at thy bosom, *clung round thee first.*
'Twas the earliest link in love's warm chain—
'Tis the only one that will long remain;
And as year by year, and day by day,
Some friend still trusted drops away,
Mother! dear mother! *oh dost thou see*
How the shorten'd chain brings me nearer thee!

PHILIP SLINGSBY.

'Tis midnight the lone mountains on—
The East is fleck'd with cloudy bars,
And, gliding through them one by one,
The moon walks up her path of stars—
The light upon her placid brow
Borrowed of fountains unseen now.

And happiness is mine to-night,
  Thus springing from an unseen fount,
And breast and brain are warm with light,
  With midnight round me on the mount—
Its rays, like thine, fair Dian, flow
From far that Western star below.

Dear mother! in thy love I live;
  The life thou gav'st flows yet from thee—
And, sun-like, thou hast power to give
  Life to the earth, air, sea, for me!
Though wandering, as this moon above,
I'm dark without thy constant love.

TO ERMENGARDE.

I KNOW not if the sunshine waste—
  The world is dark since thou art gone!
The hours are, oh! so leaden-paced!
  The birds sing, and the stars float on,
But sing not well, and look not fair—
A weight is in the summer air,
  And sadness in the sight of flowers,
And if I go where others smile,
  Their love but makes me think of ours,
And heaven gets my heart the while.
Like one upon a desert isle,
  I languish of the weary hours;
I never thought a life could be
So flung upon one hope, as mine, dear love, on thee!

I sit and watch the summer sky,
  There comes a cloud through heaven alone,
A thousand stars are shining nigh—
  It feels no light, but darkles on!
Yet now it nears the lovelier moon,
  And, flushing through its fringe of snow,
There steals a rosier die, and soon
  Its bosom is one fiery glow!
The queen of life within it lies!
  Yet mark how lovers meet to part!
The cloud already onward flies,
  And shadows sink into its heart,
And (dost thou see them where thou art?)
  Fade fast, fade all those glorious dyes!
Its light, like mine, is seen no more,
And, like my own, its heart seems darker than before!

Where press this hour those fairy feet,
  Where look this hour those eyes of blue!
What music in thine ear is sweet!
  What odor breathes thy lattice through!
What word is on thy lip? What tone—
What look—replying to thine own?

Thy steps along the Danube stray—
  Alas it seeks an orient sea!
Thou would'st not seem so far away
  Flow'd but its waters back to me?
I bless the slowly coming moon
  Because its eye look'd late in thine!
I envy the west wind of June
  Whose wings will bear it up the Rhine;
The flower I press upon my brow
Were sweeter if its like perfumed thy chamber now!

THE SHUNAMITE.*

It was a sultry day of summer time.
The sun pour'd down upon the ripen'd grain
With quivering heat, and the suspended leaves
Hung motionless. The cattle on the hills
Stood still, and the divided flock were all
Laying their nostrils to the cooling roots,
And the sky look'd like silver, and it seem'd
As if the air had fainted, and the pulse
Of nature had run down, and ceas'd to beat.

"Haste thee, my child!" the Syrian mother said,
"Thy father is athirst"—and from the depths
Of the cool well under the leaning tree,

* 2 Kings iv. 18—37.

She drew refreshing water, and with thoughts
Of God's sweet goodness stirring at her heart,
She bless'd her beautiful boy, and to his way
Committed him. And he went lightly on,
With his soft hands press'd closely to the cool
Stone vessel, and his little naked feet
Lifted with watchful care, and o'er the hills,
And through the light green hollows, where the lambs
Go for the tender grass, he kept his way,
Wiling its distance with his simple thoughts,
Till, in the wilderness of sheaves, with brows
Throbbing with heat, he set his burthen down.

Childhood is restless ever, and the boy
Stay'd not within the shadow of the tree,
But with a joyous industry went forth
Into the reapers' places, and bound up
His tiny sheaves, and plaited cunningly
The pliant withs out of the shining straw,
Cheering their labor on, till they forgot
The very weariness of their stooping toil
In the beguiling of his earnest mirth.
Presently he was silent, and his eye

Closed as with dizzy pain, and with his hand
Press'd hard upon his forehead, and his breast
Heaving with the suppression of a cry,
He utter'd a faint murmur, and fell back
Upon the loosen'd sheaf, insensible.

They bore him to his mother, and he lay
Upon her knees till noon—and then he died!
She had watch'd every breath, and kept her hand
Soft on his forehead, and gaz'd in upon
The dreamy languor of his listless eye,
And she had laid back all his sunny curls
And kiss'd his delicate lip, and lifted him
Into her bosom, till her heart grew strong—
His beauty was so unlike death! She leaned
Over him now, that she might catch the low
Sweet music of his breath, that she had learn'd
To love when he was slumbering at her side
In his unconscious infancy—

—"So still!
'Tis a soft sleep! How beautiful he lies,
With his fair forehead, and the rosy veins
Playing so freshly in his sunny cheek!

How could they say that he would die! Oh God!
I could not loose him! I have treasured all
His childhood in my heart, and even now,
As he has slept, my memory has been there,
Counting like treasure all his winning ways—
His unforgotten sweetness:—
—"Yet so still!—
How like this breathless slumber is to death!
I could believe that in that bosom now
There were no pulse—it beats so languidly!
I cannot see it stir; but his red lip!—
Death would not be so very beautiful!
And that half smile—would death have left *that* there?
—And should I not have felt that he would die?
And have I not wept over him?—and prayed
Morning and night for him?—and *could* he die?
—No—God will keep him! He will be my pride
Many long years to come, and this fair hair
Will darken like his father's, and his eye
Be of a deeper blue when he is grown;
And he will be so tall, and I shall look
With such a pride upon him!—*He* to die!"
And the fond mother lifted his soft curls,

And smiled, as if 'twere mockery to think
That such fair things could perish—
—Suddenly
Her hand shrunk from him, and the color fled
From her fix'd lip, and her supporting knees
Were shook beneath her child. Her hand had touch'd
His forehead, as she dallied with his hair—
And it was cold—like clay! Slow, very slow,
Came the misgiving that her child was dead.
She sat a moment, and her eyes were clos'd
In a dumb prayer for strength, and then she took
His little hand and press'd it earnestly—
And put her lip to his—and look'd again
Fearfully on him—and then, bending low,
She whisper'd in his ear, " My son!—My son!"
And as the echo died, and not a sound
Broke on the stillness, and he lay there still
Motionless on her knee—the truth *would* come!
And with a sharp, quick cry, as if her heart
Were crush'd, she lifted him and held him close
Into her bosom—with a mother's thought—
As if death had no power to touch him there!

* * * * *

The man of God came forth, and led the child
Unto his mother, and went on his way.
And he was there—her beautiful—her own—
Living and smiling on her—with his arms
Folded about her neck, and his warm breath
Breathing upon her lips, and in her ear
The music of his gentle voice once more!

ABSALOM.

THE waters slept. Night's silvery veil hung low
On Jordan's bosom, and the eddies curled
Their glassy rings beneath it, like the still,
Unbroken beating of the sleeper's pulse.
The reeds bent down the stream; the willow leaves,
With a soft cheek upon the lulling tide,
Forgot the lifting winds; and the long stems,
Whose flowers the water, like a gentle nurse,
Bears on its bosom, quietly gave way,
And leaned, in graceful attitudes, to rest.
How strikingly the course of nature tells,
By its light heed of human suffering,
That it was fashioned for a happier world!

King David's limbs were weary. He had fled
From far Jerusalem ; and now he stood,
With his faint people, for a little rest
Upon the shore of Jordan. The light wind
Of morn was stirring, and he bared his brow
To its refreshing breath ; for he had worn
The mourner's covering, and he had not felt
That he could see his people until now.
They gather'd round him on the fresh green bank,
And spoke their kindly words ; and, as the sun
Rose up in heaven, he knelt among them there,
And bowed his head upon his hands to pray.
Oh ! when the heart is full—when bitter thoughts
Come crowding thickly up for utterance,
And the poor common words of courtesy
Are such a very mockery—how much
The bursting heart may pour itself in prayer !
He pray'd for Israel—and his voice went up
Strongly and fervently. He pray'd for those
Whose love had been his shield—and his deep tones
Grew tremulous. But, oh ! for Absalom—
For his estranged, misguided Absalom—
The proud, bright being, who had burst away

In all his princely beauty, to defy
The heart that cherished him—for him he poured,
In agony that would not be controlled,
Strong supplication, and forgave him there,
Before his God, for his deep sinfulness.

* * * * *

The pall was settled. He who slept beneath
Was straightened for the grave ; and, as the folds
Sunk to the still proportions, they betrayed
The matchless symmetry of Absalom.
His hair was yet unshorn, and silken curls
Were floating round the tassels as they swayed
To the admitted air, as glossy now
As when, in hours of gentle dalliance, bathing
The snowy fingers of Judea's daughters.
His helm was at his feet: his banner, soiled
With trailing through Jerusalem, was laid,
Reversed, beside him: and the jewelled hilt,
Whose diamonds lit the passage of his blade,
Rested, like mockery, on his covered brow.
The soldiers of the king trod to and fro,
Clad in the garb of battle ; and their chief,
The mighty Joab, stood beside the bier,

And gazed upon the dark pall steadfastly,
As if he feared the slumberer might stir.
A slow step startled him. He grasped his blade
As if a trumpet rang; but the bent form
Of David entered, and he gave command,
In a low tone, to his few followers,
And left him with his dead. The king stood still
Till the last echo died: then, throwing off
The sackcloth from his brow, and laying back
The pall from the still features of his child,
He bowed his head upon him, and broke forth
In the resistless eloquence of wo:

"Alas! my noble boy! that thou should'st die!
  Thou, who wert made so beautifully fair!
That death should settle in thy glorious eye,
  And leave his stillness in this clustering hair!
How could he mark thee for the silent tomb,
    My proud boy, Absalom!

"Cold is thy brow, my son! and I am chill,
  As to my bosom I have tried to press thee!
How was I wont to feel my pulses thrill,

Like a rich harp-string, yearning to caress thee,
And hear thy sweet "*my father!*" from these dumb
And cold lips, Absalom!

"The grave hath won thee. I shall hear the gush
Of music, and the voices of the young;
And life will pass me in the mantling blush,
And the dark tresses to the soft winds flung;—
But thou no more, with thy sweet voice, shalt come
To meet me, Absalom!

"And oh! when I am stricken, and my heart,
Like a bruised reed, is waiting to be broken,
How will its love for thee, as I depart,
Yearn for thine ear to drink its last deep token!
It were so sweet, amid death's gathering gloom,
To see thee, Absalom!

"And now, farewell! 'Tis hard to give thee up,
With death so like a gentle slumber on thee;—
And thy dark sin!—Oh! I could drink the cup,
If from this wo its bitterness had won thee.

May God have called thee, like a wanderer, home,
My erring Absalom!"

He covered up his face, and bowed himself
A moment on his child: then, giving him
A look of melting tenderness, he clasped
His hands convulsively, as if in prayer;
And, as a strength were given him of God,
He rose up calmly, and composed the pall
Firmly and decently, and left him there,
As if his rest had been a breathing sleep.

HAGAR IN THE WILDERNESS.

THE morning broke. Light stole upon the clouds
With a strange beauty. Earth received again
Its garment of a thousand dies ; and leaves,
And delicate blossoms, and the painted flowers,
And every thing that bendeth to the dew,
And stirreth with the daylight, lifted up
Its beauty to the breath of that sweet morn.

All things are dark to sorrow ; and the light
And loveliness, and fragrant air were sad
To the dejected Hagar. The moist earth
Was pouring odours from its spicy pores,
And the young birds were singing as if life

Were a new thing to them ; but oh! it came
Upon her heart like discord, and she felt
How cruelly it tries a broken heart,
To see a mirth in any thing it loves.
She stood at Abraham's tent. Her lips were pressed
Till the blood started ; and the wandering veins
Of her transparent forehead were swelled out,
As if her pride would burst them. Her dark eye
Was clear and tearless, and the light of heaven,
Which made its language legible, shot back,
From her long lashes, as it had been flame.
Her noble boy stood by her, with his hand
Clasped in her own, and his round, delicate feet,
Scarce trained to balance on the tented floor,
Sandaled for journeying. He had looked up
Into his mother's face until he caught
The spirit there, and his young heart was swelling
Beneath his dimpled bosom, and his form
Straightened up proudly in his tiny wrath,
As if his light proportions would have swelled,
Had they but matched his spirit, to the man.

Why bends the patriarch as he cometh now
Upon his staff so wearily ? His beard

Is low upon his breast, and on his high brow,
So written with the converse of his God,
Beareth the swollen vein of agony.
His lip is quivering, and his wonted step
Of vigor is not there ; and, though the morn
Is passing fair and beautiful, he breathes
Its freshness as it were a pestilence.
Oh! man may bear with suffering: his heart
Is a strong thing, and godlike in the grasp
Of pain that wrings mortality ; but tear
One chord affection clings to, part one tie
That binds him to a woman's delicate love,
And his great spirit yieldeth like a reed.

He gave to her the water and the bread,
But spoke no word, and trusted not himself
To look upon her face, but laid his hand
In silent blessing on the fair-haired boy,
And left her to her lot of loneliness.

Should Hagar weep? May slighted woman turn,
And, as a vine the oak hath shaken off,
Bend lightly to her leaning trust again?

O no! by all her loveliness—by all
That makes life poetry and beauty, no!
Make her a slave; steal from her rosy cheek
By needless jealousies; let the last star
Leave her a watcher by your couch of pain;
Wrong her by petulance, suspicion, all
That makes her cup a bitterness—yet give
One evidence of love, and earth has not
An emblem of devotedness like hers.
But oh! estrange her once—it boots not how—
By wrong or silence, any thing that tells
A change has come upon your tenderness,—
And there is not a high thing out of heaven
Her pride o'ermastereth not.

She went her way with a strong step and slow;
Her pressed lip arched, and her clear eye undimmed,
As it had been a diamond, and her form
Borne proudly up, as if her heart breathed through.
Her child kept on in silence, though she pressed
His hand till it was pained: for he had caught,
As I have said, her spirit, and the seed
Of a stern nation had been breathed upon.

The morning past, and Asia's sun rode up
In the clear heaven, and every beam was heat.
The cattle of the hills were in the shade,
And the bright plumage of the Orient lay
On beating bosoms in her spicy trees.
It was an hour of rest; but Hagar found
No shelter in the wilderness, and on
She kept her weary way, until the boy
Hung down his head, and opened his parched lips
For water; but she could not give it him.
She laid him down beneath the sultry sky,—
For it was better than the close, hot breath
Of the thick pines,—and tried to comfort him;
But he was sore athirst, and his blue eyes,
Were dim and bloodshot, and he could not know
Why God denied him water in the wild.
She sat a little longer, and he grew
Ghastly and faint, as if he would have died.
It was too much for her. She lifted him,
And bore him farther on, and laid his head
Beneath the shadow of a desert shrub;
And, shrouding up her face, she went away,
And sat to watch, where he could see her not,

Till he should die; and, watching him, she mourned:—

"God stay thee in thine agony, my boy!
I cannot see thee die; I cannot brook
Upon thy brow to look,
And see death settle on my cradle joy.
How have I drunk the light of thy blue eye!
And could I see thee die?

"I did not dream of this when thou wast straying,
Like an unbound gazelle, among the flowers;
Or wearing rosy hours,
By the rich gush of water-sources playing,
Then sinking weary to thy smiling sleep,
So beautiful and deep.

"Oh no! and when I watched by thee the while,
And saw thy bright lip curling in thy dream,
And thought of the dark stream
In my own land of Egypt, the far Nile,
How prayed I that my father's land might be
An heritage for thee!

"And now the grave for its cold breast hath won thee,
And thy white, delicate limbs the earth will press;
        And oh! my last caress
Must feel thee cold, for a chill hand is on thee.
How can I leave my boy, so pillowed there
        Upon his clustering hair!"

She stood beside the well her God had given
To gush in that deep wilderness, and bathed
The forehead of her child until he laughed
In his reviving happiness, and lisped
His infant thought of gladness at the sight
Of the cool plashing of his mother's hand.

THE WIDOW OF NAIN.*

The Roman sentinel stood helmed and tall
Beside the gate of Nain. The busy tread
Of comers to the city mart was done,
For it was almost noon, and a dead heat
Quiver'd upon the fine and sleeping dust,
And the cold snake crept panting from the wall,
And bask'd his scaly circles in the sun.
Upon his spear the soldier lean'd, and kept
His idle watch, and, as his drowsy dream
Was broken by the solitary foot
Of some poor mendicant, he rais'd his head
To curse him for a tributary Jew,
And slumberously dozed on.

* Luke, chap. vii.

'Twas now high noon.
The dull, low murmur of a funeral
Went through the city—the sad sound of feet
Unmix'd with voices—and the sentinel
Shook off his slumber, and gazed earnestly
Up the wide street along whose pavéd way
The silent throng crept slowly. They came on,
Bearing a body heavily on its bier,
And by the crowd that in the burning sun
Walk'd with forgetful sadness, 'twas of one
Mourn'd with uncommon sorrow. The broad gate
Swung on its hinges, and the Roman bent
His spear-point downwards as the bearers past
Bending beneath their burthen. There was one—
Only one mourner. Close behind the bier
Crumpling the pall up in her wither'd hands,
Follow'd an aged woman. Her short steps
Falter'd with weakness, and a broken moan
Fell from her lips, thicken'd convulsively
As her heart bled afresh. The pitying crowd
Follow'd apart, but no one spoke to her.
She had no kinsmen. She had lived alone—
A widow with one son. He was her all—

The only tie she had in the wide world—
And he was dead. They could not comfort her.

Jesus drew near to Nain as from the gate
The funeral came forth. His lips were pale
With the noon's sultry heat. The beaded sweat
Stood thickly on his brow, and on the worn
And simple latchets of his sandals lay
Thick the white dust of travel. He had come
Since sunrise from Capernaum, staying not
To wet his lips by green Bethsaida's pool,
Nor wash his feet in Kishon's silver springs,
Nor turn him southward upon Tabor's side
To catch Gilboa's light and spicy breeze.
Genesareth stood cool upon the East,
Fast by the sea of Galilee, and there
The weary traveller might bide till eve,
And on the alders of Bethulia's plains
The grapes of Palestine hung ripe and wild,
Yet turn'd he not aside, but gazing on
From every swelling mount, he saw afar
Amid the hills the humble spires of Nain,
The place of his next errand, and the path

Touch'd not Bethulia, and a league away
Upon the East lay pleasant Galilee.

Forth from the city-gate the pitying crowd
Follow'd the stricken mourner. They came near
The place of burial, and, with straining hands,
Closer upon her breast she clasp'd the pall,
And with a gasping sob, quick as a child's,
And an inquiring wildness flashing through
The thin, gray lashes of her fever'd eyes,
She came where Jesus stood beside the way.
He look'd upon her, and his heart was moved.
"Weep not!" he said, and, as they stay'd the bier,
And at his bidding laid it at his feet,
He gently drew the pall from out her grasp
And laid it back in silence from the dead.
With troubled wonder the mute throng drew near,
And gaz'd on his calm looks. A minute's space
He stood and pray'd. Then taking the cold hand
He said, "Arise!" And instantly the breast
Heav'd in its cerements, and a sudden flush
Ran through the lines of the divided lips,

And, with a murmur of his mother's name,
He trembled and sat upright in his shroud.
And, while the mourner hung upon his neck,
Jesus went calmly on his way to Nain.

DAWN.

> "*That* line I learned not in the old sad song."
>
> CHARLES LAMB.

THROW up the window! 'Tis a morn for life
In its most subtle luxury. The air
Is like a breathing from a rarer world;
And the south wind is like a gentle friend,
Parting the hair so softly on my brow.
It has come over gardens, and the flowers
That kissed it are betrayed; for as it parts,
With its invisible fingers, my loose hair,
I know it has been trifling with the rose,
And stooping to the violet. There is joy
For all God's creatures in it. The wet leaves

Are stirring at its touch, and birds are singing
As if to breathe were music, and the grass
Sends up its modest odor with the dew,
Like the small tribute of humility.

I had awoke from an unpleasant dream,
And light was welcome to me. I looked out
To feel the common air, and when the breath
Of the delicious morning met my brow
Cooling its fever, and the pleasant sun
Shone on familiar objects, it was like
The feeling of the captive who comes forth
From darkness to the cheerful light of day.
Oh! could we wake from sorrow; were it all
A troubled dream like this, to cast aside
Like an untimely garment with the morn;
Could the long fever of the heart be cooled
By a sweet breath from nature; or the gloom
Of a bereaved affection pass away
With looking on the lively tint of flowers—
How lightly were the spirit reconciled,
To make this beautiful, bright world its home!

SATURDAY AFTERNOON.

(A PICTURE.)

I LOVE to look on a scene like this,
  Of wild and careless play,
And persuade myself that I am not old,
  And my locks are not yet gray;
For it stirs the blood in an old man's heart,
  And makes his pulses fly,
To catch the thrill of a happy voice,
  And the light of a pleasant eye.

I have walked the world for fourscore years;
  And they say that I am old,
And my heart is ripe for the reaper, Death,
  And my years are well nigh told.

It is very true ; it is very true ;
  I'm old, and " I 'bide my time :"
But my heart will leap at a scene like this
  And I half renew my prime.

Play on, play on ; I am with you there,
  In the midst of your merry ring ;
I can feel the thrill of the daring jump,
  And rush of the breathless swing.
I hide with you in the fragrant hay,
  And I whoop the smothered call,
And my feet slip up on the seedy floor,
  And I care not for the fall.

I am willing to die when my time shall come,
  And I shall be glad to go ;
For the world at best is a weary place,
  And my pulse is getting low ;
But the grave is dark, and the heart will fail
  In treading its gloomy way ;
And it wiles my heart from its dreariness,
  To see the young so gay.

A CHILD'S FIRST IMPRESSION OF A STAR.

SHE had been told that God made all the stars
That twinkled up in heaven, and now she stood
Watching the coming of the twilight on,
As if it were a new and perfect world,
And this were its first eve. She stood alone
By the low window, with the silken lash
Of her soft eye upraised, and her sweet mouth
Half parted with the new and strange delight
Of beauty that she could not comprehend,
And had not seen before. The purple folds
Of the low sunset clouds, and the blue sky
That looked so still and delicate above,
Filled her young heart with gladness, and the eve
Stole on with its deep shadows, and she still

Stood looking at the west with that half-smile,
As if a pleasant thought were at her heart.
Presently, in the edge of the last tint
Of sunset, where the blue was melted in
To the faint golden mellowness, a star
Stood suddenly. A laugh of wild delight
Burst from her lips, and putting up her hands,
Her simple thought broke forth expressively—
" Father, dear father, God has made a star!"

MAY.

Oh the merry May has pleasant hours,
  And dreamily they glide,
As if they floated like the leaves
  Upon a silver tide.
The trees are full of crimson buds,
  And the woods are full of birds,
And the waters flow to music
  Like a tune with pleasant words.

The verdure of the meadow-land
  Is creeping to the hills,
The sweet, blue-bosom'd violets
  Are blooming by the rills ;

The lilac has a load of balm
  For every wind that stirs,
And the larch stands green and beautiful
  Amid the sombre firs.

There's perfume upon every wind—
  Music in every tree—
Dews for the moisture-loving flowers—
  Sweets for the sucking bee ;
The sick come forth for the healing breeze,
  The young are gathering flowers ;
And life is a tale of poetry,
  That is told by golden hours.

If 'tis not true philosophy,
  That the spirit when set free
Still lingers about its olden home,
  In the flower and the tree,
It is very strange that our pulses thrill
  At the tint of a voiceless thing,
And our hearts yearn so with tenderness
  In the beautiful time of Spring.

ON WITNESSING A BAPTISM.

SHE stood up in the meekness of a heart
Resting on God, and held her fair young child
Upon her bosom, with its gentle eyes
Folded in sleep, as if its soul had gone
To whisper the baptismal vow in heaven.
The prayer went up devoutly, and the lips
Of the good man glowed fervently with faith
That it would be, even as he had pray'd,
And the sweet child be gather'd to the fold
Of Jesus. As the holy words went on
Her lips mov'd silently, and tears, fast tears,
Stole from beneath her lashes, and upon
The forehead of the beautiful child lay soft
With the baptismal water. Then I thought

That, to the eye of God, that mother's tears
Would be a deeper covenant, which sin
And the temptations of the world, and death,
Would leave unbroken, and that she would know
In the clear light of heaven, how very strong
The prayer which press'd them from her heart had
been
In leading its young spirit up to God.

THE ANNOYER.

> "Common as light is love,
> And its familiar voice wearies not ever."
>
> SHELLEY.

Love knoweth every form of air,
  And every shape of earth,
And comes, unbidden, everywhere,
  Like thought's mysterious birth.
The moonlit sea and the sunset sky
  Are written with Love's words,
And you hear his voice unceasingly,
  Like song in the time of birds.

He peeps into the warrior's heart

From the tip of a stooping plume,
And the serried spears, and the many men
May not deny him room.
He'll come to his tent in the weary night,
And be busy in his dream ;
And he'll float to his eye in morning light
Like a fay on a silver beam.

He hears the sound of the hunter's gun,
And rides on the echo back,
And sighs in his ear, like a stirring leaf,
And flits in his woodland track.
The shade of the wood, and the sheen of the river
The cloud, and the open sky—
He will haunt them all with his subtle quiver,
Like the light of your very eye.

The fisher hangs over the leaning boat,
And ponders the silver sea,
For Love is under the surface hid,
And a spell of thought has he,
He heaves the wave like a bosom sweet,
And speaks in the ripple low,

Till the bait is gone from the crafty line,
  And the hook hangs bare below.

He blurs the print of the scholar's book,
  And intrudes in the maiden's prayer,
And profanes the cell of the holy man,
  In the shape of a lady fair.
In the darkest night, and the bright daylight,
  In earth, and sea, and sky,
In every home of human thought,
  Will love be lurking nigh.

ROARING BROOK.

(A PASSAGE OF SCENERY IN CONNECTICUT.)

It was a mountain stream that with the leap
Of its impatient waters had worn out
A channel in the rock, and wash'd away
The earth that had upheld the tall old trees,
Till it was darken'd with the shadowy arch
Of the o'er-leaning branches. Here and there
It loiter'd in a broad and limpid pool
That circled round demurely, and anon
Sprung violently over where the rock
Fell suddenly, and bore its bubbles on,
Till they were broken by the hanging moss,
As anger with a gentle word grows calm.
In spring-time, when the snows were coming down,

And in the flooding of the Autumn rains,
No foot might enter there—but in the hot
And thirsty summer, when the fountains slept,
You could go up its channel in the shade,
To the far sources, with a brow as cool
As in the grotto of the anchorite.
Here when an idle student have I come,
And in a hollow of the rock lain down
And mus'd until the eventide, or read
Some fine old poet till my nook became
A haunt of faery, or the busy flow
Of water to my spell-bewilder'd ear
Seem'd like the din of some gay tournament.
Pleasant have been such hours, and tho' the wise
Have said that I was indolent, and they
Who taught me have reprov'd me that I play'd
The truant in the leafy month of June,
I deem it true philosophy in him
Whose path is in the rude and busy world,
To loiter with these wayside comforters.

LINES ON THE NEW YEAR.

JANUARY 1, 1825.

FLEETLY hath past the year. The seasons came
Duly as they are wont—the gentle Spring,
And the delicious Summer, and the cool,
Rich Autumn, with the nodding of the grain,
And Winter, like an old and hoary man,
Frosty and stiff—and so are chronicled—
We have found beauty in the new green leaf,
And in the first blown violets; we have drunk
Cool water from the rock, and in the shade
Sunk to the noon-tide slumber;—we have eat
The mellow fruitage of the bending tree,
And girded to our pleasant wanderings
When the cool wind came freshly from the hills;

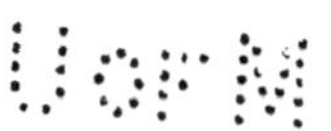

And when the tinting of the Autumn leaves
Had faded from its glory, we have sat
By the good fires of Winter, and rejoiced
Over the fulness of the gathered sheaf.
" God hath been good to us!" 'Tis He whose hand
Moulded the sunny hills, and hollowed out
The shelter of the valleys, and doth keep
The fountains in their secret places cool;
And it is He who leadeth up the sun
And ordereth the starry influences,
And tempereth the keenness of the frost—
And therefore, in the plenty of the feast,
And in the lifting of the cup, let HIM
Have praises for the well completed year.

LINES ON THE NEW YEAR.

JANUARY 1, 1826.

WINTER is come again. The sweet south-west
Is a forgotten wind, and the strong earth
Has laid aside its mantle to be bound
By the frost fetter. There is not a sound,
Save of the skaiter's heel, and there is laid
An icy finger on the lip of streams,
And the clear icicle hangs cold and still,
And the snow-fall is noiseless as a thought,
Spring has a rushing sound, and Summer sends
Many sweet voices with its odors out,
And Autumn rustleth its decaying robe
With a complaining whisper. Winter's dumb!
God made his ministry a silent one,

And he has given him a foot of steel
And an unlovely aspect, and a breath
Sharp to the senses—and we know that He
Tempereth well, and hath a meaning hid
Under the shadow of his hand. Look up!
And it shall be interpreted. Your home
Hath a temptation now. There is no voice
Of waters with beguiling for your ear,
And the cool forest and the meadows green
Witch not your feet away; and in the dells
There are no violets, and upon the hills
There are no sunny places to lie down.
You must go in, and by your cheerful fire
Wait for the offices of love, and hear
Accents of human tenderness, and feast
Your eye upon the beauty of the young.
It is a season for the quiet thought,
And the still reckoning with thyself. The year
Gives back the spirits of its dead, and time
Whispers the history of its vanished hours;
And the heart, calling its affections up,
Counteth its wasted treasure. Life stands still

And settles like a fountain, and the eye
Sees clearly through its depths, and noteth all
That stirred its troubled waters. It is well
That Winter with the dying year should come!

ON THE DEATH OF A YOUNG GIRL.

'Tis difficult to feel that she is dead.
Her presence, like the shadow of a wing
That is just lessening in the upper sky,
Lingers upon us. We can hear her voice,
And for her step we listen, and the eye
Looks for her wonted coming with a strange,
Forgetful earnestness. We cannot feel
That she will no more come—that from her cheek
The delicate flush has faded, and the light
Dead in her soft dark eye, and on her lip,
That was so exquisitely pure, the dew
Of the damp grave has fallen! Who, so lov'd,
Is left among the living? Who hath walk'd
The world with such a winning loveliness,

And on its bright brief journey, gather'd up
Such treasures of affection? She was lov'd
Only as idols are. She was the pride
Of her familiar sphere—the daily joy
Of all who on her gracefulness might gaze,
And in the light and music of her way,
Have a companion's portion. Who could feel
While looking upon beauty such as hers,
That it would ever perish! It is like
The melting of a star into the sky
While you are gazing on it, or a dream
In its most ravishing sweetness rudely broken.

ANDRE'S REQUEST TO WASHINGTON.

It is not the fear of death
 That damps my brow
It is not for another breath
 I ask thee now ;
I can die with a lip unstirr'd
 And a quiet heart—
Let but this prayer be heard
 Ere I depart.

I can give up my mother's look—
 My sister's kiss ;
I can think of love—yet brook
 A death like this !
I can give up the young fame

I burn'd to win—
All—but the spotless name
I glory in.

Thine is the power to give,
Thine to deny,
Joy for the hour I live—
Calmness to die.
By all the brave should cherish,
By my dying breath,
I ask that I may perish
By a soldier's death !

SONNET—WINTER.

The frozen ground looks gray. 'Twill shut the snow
Out from its bosom, and the flakes will fall
Softly, and lie upon it. The hushed flow
Of the ice-covered waters, and the call
Of the cold driver to his oxen slow,
And the complaining of the gust, are all
That I can hear of music—would that I
With the green summer like a leaf might die!
So will a man grow gray, and on his head
The snow of years lie visibly, and so
Will come a frost when his green years have fled
And his chilled pulses sluggishly will flow,
And his deep voice be shaken—would that I
In the green summer of my youth might die!

SONNET.

Storm had been on the hills. The day had worn
  As if a sleep upon the hours had crept;
And the dark clouds that gather'd at the morn
  In dull, impenetrable masses slept,
And the wet leaves hung droopingly, and all
Was like the mournful aspect of a pall.
  Suddenly on the horizon's edge a blue
And delicate line, as of a pencil, lay,
  And as it wider and intenser grew,
The darkness removed silently away,
  And, with the splendor of a God, broke through
The perfect glory of departing day—
So, when his stormy pilgrimage is o'er,
Will light upon the dying Christian pour.

SONNET.

Beautiful robin! with thy feathers red
  Contrasting sweetly with the soft green tree,
Making thy little flights as thou art led
  By things that tempt a simple one like thee—
I would that thou couldst warble me to tears
As lightly as the birds of other years!
  Idly to lie beneath an April sun,
Pressing the perfume from the tender grass;
  To watch a joyous rivulet leap on
With the clear tinkle of a music glass,
And as I saw the early robin pass,
  To hear him thro' his little compass run—
Hath been a joy that I shall no more know
Before I to my better portion go.

THE TABLE OF EMERALD.

"Deep, it is said, under yonder pyramid, has for ages lain concealed the Table of Emerald, on which the thrice-great Hermes engraved before the flood the secret of alchemy that gives gold at will."

MOORE'S EPICUREAN.

THAT Emerald vast of the Pyramid—
Were I where it is laid,
I would ask no king for his weary crown,
As its mystic words were said.
The pomp of wealth, the show of power,
In vain for me would shine,
And nought that brings the mind a care,
Would win bright gold of mine.

Would I feast all day—revel all night—
  Laugh with a secret sadness?
Would I sleep away the breezy morn,
  And wake to the goblet's madness?
Would I spend no time and no golden ore
  For the wisdom that sages knew?
Would I run to waste with a human mind
  To its holy trust untrue?

Oh! knew I the depth of that emerald spell,
  And had I the gold it brings,
I would never load with a mocking joy
  My spirit's mounting wings.
I would bind no wreath to my brow to day
  That would leave a stain to-morrow,
Nor drink a draught of joy to-night,
  That would change with morn to sorrow.

But, oh, I would burst this chain of care,
  And be spirit and fancy-free;
My mind should range where it longs to go
  And the limitless wind outflee.
I would place my foot on my heaps of ore

To mount to Wisdom's throne,
And buy, with the wealth of an Indian mine,
To be left, of care, alone!

Ambition! my lip would laugh to scorn
Thy robe and thy gleaming sword!
I would follow sooner a woman's eye,
Or a child's imperfect word;
But come with the glory of human thought,
And the light of the scholar's brow,
And my heart shall be taught forgetfulness,
And alone at thine altar bow.

There was one mild eye—there was one deep tone—
They were dear to this heart of mine!
Dearer to me was that mild blue eye
Than the lamp on wisdom's shrine.
My soul brought up from its deepest cell
The sum of its earthly love;
But it could not buy her wing from Heaven,
And she flew to her rest above.

That first deep love I have taken back

In my rayless breast to hide;
With the tear it brought for a burning seal
'Twill there forever bide.
I may stretch on now to another goal,
I may feed my thoughts of flame—
The tie is broken that kept me back,
And my mind speeds on—for fame!

But, alas! I am dreaming as if I knew
The spell of the tablet green!
I forget how like to a broken reed
Is the hope on which I lean.
There is nothing true of my idle dream
But the wreck of my early love,
And my mind is coin'd for my daily bread,
And how can it soar above?

THE END.

IV.

Mrs. Jameson's Illustrated Work.

CHARACTERISTICS OF WOMEN:

MORAL, POETICAL AND HISTORICAL.

BY MRS. JAMESON.

Illustrated by a series of her own Vignette Etchings.

V.

Mrs. Shelley's New Work.

FALKNER—A NOVEL.

BY MRS. SHELLEY.

Authoress of "Frankenstein," &c.

VI.

Mr. Grant's New Work.

THE GREAT METROPOLIS.

BY THE AUTHOR OF

"Random Recollections of the Lords and Commons," &c.

Fourth Edition.

VII.

Mr. Bulwer's New Drama:

THE DUCHESS DE LA VALLIERE

A Play in Five Acts.

Second Edition.

VIII.

Mr. Willis's New Work.

INKLINGS OF ADVENTURE.

BY N. P. WILLIS, ESQ.

Third Edition.

www.ingramcontent.com/pod-product-compliance
Lightning Source LLC
LaVergne TN
LVHW010253110826
845151LV00004B/1465

* 9 7 8 1 4 2 5 5 2 2 0 8 7 *